CHRISTMAS COOKIES

GOOD
HOUSEKEEPING

CHRISTMAS COOKIES

75 IRRESISTIBLE HOLIDAY TREATS

★ GOOD FOOD GUARANTEED ★

HEARST
books

HEARSTBOOKS

An Imprint of Sterling Publishing Co., Inc.
1166 Avenue of the Americas
New York, NY 10036

ISBN 978-1-61837-145-4

The Good Housekeeping Cookbook Seal guarantees that the recipes in this cookbook meet
the strict standards of the Good Housekeeping Research Institute. The Institute has been a source of
reliable information and a consumer advocate since 1900, and established its seal of approval in 1909.
Every recipe has been triple-tested for ease, reliability, and great taste.

Distributed in Canada by Sterling Publishing
c/o Canadian Manda Group, 664 Annette Street
Toronto, Ontario, Canada M6S 2C8

www.goodhousekeeping.com

For information about custom editions, special sales, and premium and corporate purchases,
please contact Sterling Special Sales at 800-805-5489 or specialsales@sterlingpublishing.com.

Manufactured in China

2 4 6 8 10 9 7 5 3 1

www.sterlingpublishing.com

GOOD HOUSEKEEPING
Jane Francisco
EDITOR IN CHIEF
Melissa Geurts
DESIGN DIRECTOR
Susan Westmoreland
FOOD DIRECTOR

Cover Design: Laura Palese
Interior Design: Barbara Balch
Project Editor: Carol Prager

CONTENTS

Chocolate-Dipped Peppermint
Sticks (page 23)

Foreword

Growing up, getting ready for Christmas meant lots of cookie baking. One of my earliest memories is of helping my grandmother carry pans of just-baked Mostaccioli Cookies (page 56) into her bedroom and placing them on a clean white sheet to cool. The recipe called for a 5-pound bag of flour and the bed was the only space big enough to lay out the cookies! In my house I've scaled things back a bit, but it wouldn't be Christmas without a collection of favorite cookies for celebrating and giving. Here in the Good Housekeeping Test Kitchens, the holiday countdown starts early. Even in the heat of July, the aroma of cookies baking brings a "What are you guys making?" and a smile from anyone who passes by. We always reward them with a taste of whatever is cooling, and in return, many of them have passed on to us their family's favorite cookie recipes. Sharing these sweet indulgences is as much a part of the holiday celebration as the Christmas tree.

For this book, we've collected over 70 of our all-time favorite cookie recipes: a scrumptious mix of favorite family recipes from our staff and readers, plus creative cookie recipes developed by our Test Kitchen team. We hope you'll find many of your old standbys, and discover some new ones, too.

Whether you want to bake cookie jar favorites—Easy Snickerdoodles (page 20), Chocolate Chip Jumbos (page 35); easy-to-shape cookies—Razzy-Jammy Thumbprints (page 86), PB & J Pinwheels (page 118) and biscotti —Walnut Biscotti (page 52) ; bar cookies—fruit- and nut-studded Orange-Ginger Bars (page 83), Cherry Linzer Bars (page 81), Butter-Almond Thins (page 78); or cutout cookies—sugar or gingerbread, you can bake them all with confidence. As always, every recipe in this book has been triple-tested by the Good Housekeeping Test Kitchens to ensure that it will work in any oven, with any brand of ingredient, no matter what.

SUSAN WESTMORELAND
Food Director, *Good Housekeeping*

Introduction

Cookies are a mouthwatering sweet everyone loves to eat . . . especially during the holidays. But let's face it—this is the most hectic time of year, so *Good Housekeeping Christmas Cookies* makes sure that you, the baker, take equal pleasure in making them. Whether you're an expert cookie baker or an enthusiastic beginner, our amazing recipes and treasure trove of information will ensure you bake your very best.

Top Five Tips for Cookie Bakers

To bake a perfect batch of holiday cookies, little things add up fast. So we asked the Good Housekeeping Food Department to share their secrets to sweet success.

1 Choose high-quality cookie sheets. We use heavy-gauge aluminum or heavyweight sheets with a light colored finish. Cheaper lightweight sheets can warp; dark-finished ones tend to produce cookies with overbaked bottoms and undercooked tops. Forget jelly-roll pans; your cookies won't brown evenly. Opt for a flat sheet with or without a lip (for holding) on one end. For proper heat distribution, sheets should be at least 2 inches smaller than your oven in length and width. If your sheets are old and discolored, line them with parchment paper for even browning.

2 Splurge on butter. It's interchangeable with margarine in some of our recipes, but for the best cookie flavor and texture, our advice is to stick with the real thing. Butter also enhances the flavor of other ingredients, like spices, nuts, and chocolate. If you prefer margarine, make sure it contains 80 percent fat.

3 Take measuring seriously. Our cookie recipes are exact formulas. Even ¼ teaspoon too much of baking powder could cause the dough to puff and fall, while extra flour results in stiff cookies that taste dry. Use dry measuring cups to measure dry ingredients, and liquid measuring cups for wet ingredients. Always spoon flour, confectioners' sugar, and cocoa into dry measuring cups, then level off by sweeping across the top with the back of a table knife or metal spatula. Don't pack down unless you're measuring brown sugar.

4 Avoid overmixing the dough. Unless the recipe says otherwise, mix dough only until blended after adding the flour (otherwise your cookies will be tough).

5 Check in early. No two ovens are exactly the same, so the majority of our recipes have a range of baking times. Always check cookies after the minimum time. If they're not ready, stay close to the oven for the remainder of time to avoid overbaking. Just a single extra minute can seriously compromise your hard work.

Cookie Stress Busters

Want to get a beat on holiday baking? Follow our advice and you won't get stuck in a cookie crunch.

- **Freeze your cookie dough.** Wrap it tightly in plastic wrap, then place in a freezer-weight plastic bag and freeze for up to 1 month.
  - *For rolled cookies*, like our Gingerbread Cutouts (page 16), shape dough into one or more 1-inch-thick disks. Let thaw in the fridge overnight before rolling and cutting.
  - *For drop cookies*, such as our Holiday Oatmeal Cookies (page 43), spoon dough into a plastic

Way, Way Ahead

If you plan to keep cookies for an extended period of time, don't sprinkle them with confectioners' sugar, spread them with glaze, or fill them. The sugar will be absorbed, stealing that snow-like finish, the glaze may dry or crystallize, and the jam will harden. Instead, allow some wiggle room time-wise to sprinkle, glaze, or fill your cookies right before serving or giving away.

freezer-safe container. Let thaw in the refrigerator for 1 to 2 days before baking.
- *For slice-and-bake cookies*, like our Chocolate-Citrus Cran Wheels (page 117), shape dough into logs, and then freeze. To bake, slice frozen dough, place slices on a cookie sheet, and then bake without thawing.
- **Line the cookie sheets with parchment paper,** and you won't have to clean up the sheets between batches. As one batch bakes, set up the next piece of parchment so it is ready to slide onto the next sheet.
- **Organize your decorations.** Divide colored sugar crystals and/or candies into bowls. Divide Ornamental Frosting (page 18) into bowls. Tint each portion of frosting a different color with food coloring. Use disposable piping bags or plastic food bags for easy clean up. Cover bowls of any extra frosting with plastic wrap until ready to use, as it dries up quickly.
- **Stash your baked cookies.** Place baked and completely cooled decorated cookies in airtight containers with wax paper between layers. Store at room temperature for 1 to 2 weeks and freeze up to 2 to 3 months, or as recipe directs. To defrost, just unwrap and thaw at room temperature.

Holiday Cookies Hit the Road

Nothing's sweeter than sending a batch of homemade cookies to a far-off friend or family member. However, you don't want the recipient to open a box of smashed crumbs! Our packing guidelines ensure that your treats will arrive in shipshape.
- **Opt for sturdy cookies.** (versus fragile, buttery cookies that can disintegrate en route). Drop cookies, bar cookies, and slice-and-bake cookies are the best candidates for traveling. Try our Christmas Fruit Drops (page 30), Brown Sugar-Hazelnut Bars (page 72), or PB & J Pinwheels (page 118).
- **Cushion your cookies.** Wrap cookies individually or in pairs (place the flat bottoms together) using foil, plastic wrap, or individual cellophane bags, and then place in self-sealing plastic bags.
- **Package similar cookies together.** If you're sending an assortment of cookies, wrap spice, soft, and crisp cookies separately to preserve their textures and prevent their flavors from mingling.

A Word About Chocolate

There isn't a single ingredient that can quickly transform an ordinary cookie into an extraordinary holiday treat more than chocolate.

Here are some tidbits of chocolate wisdom:

- **Store chocolate in a cool, dry place.** If stashed in a warm place (i.e., near the stove), chocolate can develop a grey-ish white "bloom" when the cocoa butter rises to the surface. Don't panic if this happens, because when chocolate is baked or melted, the bloom will vanish.

- **Know when to use chocolate chips (versus bars).** We prefer to stir in chips, which are designed to hold their shape in drop-cookie dough, like our Chocolate Chip Jumbos (page 34). Chocolate in bar form is best for melting or dipping, like our Coconut Joy Bars (page 79) or Chocolate-Almond Meringues (page 106).

- **Semisweet and bittersweet chocolate are interchangeable.** Use bittersweet chocolate if you're looking for a more intense chocolate flavor.

- **Line a sturdy container** (i.e., a small cardboard box, plastic shoebox, or metal tin) with cookie-cradling packing materials such as bubble wrap, foam peanuts, or crumpled waxed or parchment paper. Carefully nestle the cookies inside the container, and seal with tape or tie tightly with ribbon.

- **Place the container in a heavyweight cardboard shipping box.** Add enough crumpled newspaper, bubble wrap, or foam peanuts to prevent the container from shifting. Write "fragile" and "perishable" on all sides of the box.

- **Check the calendar.** Cookies shipped on a Thursday will sit in a warehouse all weekend, so mail early in the week. Or, for optimal freshness, consider springing for overnight shipping.

Butter Cookie Cutouts
(page 15)

1 | One Dough Does It

Here's a holiday plan: make our best, buttery Basic Cookie Dough, add a few twists, and you have a choice of eight fabulous Christmas cookies. If simplicity is what you seek, try our easy-bake Cranberry-Orange Spice Cookies or Chewy Fruit Bars. Or if you're feeling artsy, we've got lots of pro tips for decorated cookies, like our Butter Cookie Cutouts, Gingerbread Cutouts, and Stained Glass Ornaments that guarantee your efforts will be nothing but fun.

BASIC
Cookie Dough

Nothing but butter will do in this simple recipe. Not only does it make the best-tasting cookies, but it also ensures that the dough will be much more manageable to work with. (Margarines and spreads are often too soft to produce a cookie that can be rolled or shaped easily.)

ACTIVE TIME: 5 MINUTES   TOTAL TIME: 10 MINUTES
MAKES: 4 TO 5 DOZEN COOKIES (DEPENDING ON THE RECIPE)

2¾ cups all-purpose flour

¼ teaspoon baking soda

¼ teaspoon salt

1 cup (2 sticks) butter, softened

¾ cup granulated sugar

1 large egg

1 teaspoon vanilla extract

1 In medium bowl with wire whisk, combine flour, baking soda, and salt.

2 In large bowl with mixer on medium speed, beat butter and sugar for 1 minute or until light and fluffy, occasionally scraping bowl with rubber spatula. Add egg and vanilla; beat until well mixed. Reduce speed to low; gradually beat in flour mixture just until blended, occasionally scraping bowl.

3 Follow directions for your choice of cookie.

On a Roll

Handling cookie cutouts like our Butter Cookie Cutouts (right), Gingerbread Cutouts (page 16), or Stained Glass Ornaments (page 25) can be tricky, but we've got just the fixes for these common troubles:

- **Chilled dough is too firm to roll out.** Allow it to stand for 5 to 10 minutes at room temperature to soften slightly.

- **Dough becomes too soft during rolling.** Place in the fridge or freezer until firm and manageable again.

- **Cookie cutouts fall apart before baking.** Freeze them on waxed paper until firm, and then transfer the chilled cutouts to cookie sheets.

Butter Cookie
CUTOUTS

Here's the holiday cookie that covers all the bases: crispy, buttery, and decorated with Christmas whimsy. For photo, see page 12.

ACTIVE TIME: 30 MINUTES   **TOTAL TIME:** 1 HOUR PLUS CHILLING AND COOLING   **MAKES:** 5 DOZEN COOKIES

Basic Cookie Dough (left)

Ornamental Frosting (page 18), optional

Sugar Pearls (available at wilton.com), optional

Colored sugar crystals, optional

1 Prepare Basic Cookie Dough; divide into 3 equal pieces. Flatten each piece into a disk, and wrap each in plastic wrap. Refrigerate for at least 2 hours or overnight until dough is firm enough to roll.

2 Preheat oven to 350°F. Between two sheets of waxed paper, roll 1 disk of dough ⅛-inch thick. Remove top sheet of waxed paper. With floured 3- to 4-inch holiday-shaped cookie cutters, cut dough into as many cookies as possible; wrap and refrigerate trimmings. Place cookies, 1 inch apart, on large ungreased cookie sheet.

3 Bake for 11 to 13 minutes or until golden brown. With spatula, transfer cookies to wire racks to cool completely. Repeat with remaining dough and trimmings.

4 When cookies are cool, prepare Ornamental Frosting, if desired; use to decorate cookies. Decorate with colored sugar and Sugar Pearls, if desired. Set cookies aside to allow frosting to dry, about 1 hour.

EACH COOKIE (WITHOUT DECORATION): ABOUT 70 CALORIES, 1G PROTEIN, 9G CARBOHYDRATE, 3G TOTAL FAT (2G SATURATED), 0G FIBER, 12MG CHOLESTEROL, 50MG SODIUM.

TIP

For perfect rolled-out cookies, roll the dough on a flat, smooth surface. Sprinkle the work surface with a bit of water to prevent the waxed paper from sliding. Roll the disk of dough from the center to the edge.

Gingerbread CUTOUTS

Nothing says Christmas like gingerbread cookies,
and our version of this holiday classic is perfectly spiced
with just the right hint of molasses.

ACTIVE TIME: 30 MINUTES   **TOTAL TIME:** 1 HOUR 30 MINUTES PLUS CHILLING AND COOLING
MAKES: 5 DOZEN COOKIES

Basic Cookie Dough (page 14)

½   teaspoon baking soda

2   teaspoons ground cinnamon

2   teaspoons ground ginger

½   teaspoon ground nutmeg

¼   teaspoon ground cloves

¾   cup packed dark brown sugar

¼   cup dark molasses

Ornamental Frosting (page 18), optional

Colored sugar crystals, optional

1 Prepare Basic Cookie Dough, but in step 1, increase baking soda to ½ teaspoon total and add cinnamon, ginger, nutmeg, and cloves to flour mixture. In step 2, reduce butter to 1 stick, substitute dark brown sugar for granulated, and add molasses with egg and vanilla.

2 Divide dough into 3 equal pieces. Flatten each into a disk; wrap each in plastic wrap. Refrigerate for at least 2 hours or overnight until dough is firm enough to roll.

3 Preheat oven to 350°F. Between two sheets of waxed paper, roll 1 disk of dough ⅛-inch thick. Remove top sheet of waxed paper. With floured 3- to 4-inch holiday-shaped cookie cutters, cut out as many cookies as possible; wrap and refrigerate trimmings. Place cookies, 1 inch apart, on large ungreased cookie sheet.

4 Bake for 11 to 13 minutes or until edges begin to brown. With spatula, transfer cookies to wire racks to cool completely. Repeat with remaining dough and trimmings.

5 When cookies are cool, prepare Ornamental Frosting, if desired; use to decorate cookies. Sprinkle with colored sugar, if desired. Set cookies aside to allow frosting to dry, about 1 hour.

EACH COOKIE (WITHOUT DECORATION): ABOUT 75 CALORIES, 1G PROTEIN, 11G CARBOHYDRATE, 3G TOTAL FAT (2G SATURATED), 0G FIBER, 12MG CHOLESTEROL, 50MG SODIUM.

Ornamental FROSTING

This go-to holiday recipe is as simple as it gets.

TOTAL TIME: 10 MINUTES   MAKES: 3 CUPS

1   box (16 ounces) confectioners' sugar
3   tablespoons meringue powder
Assorted food colorings

1 In large bowl with mixer on medium speed, beat sugar, meringue powder, and ⅓ *cup warm water* until blended and mixture is very stiff, about 5 minutes.

2 Tint frosting with food colorings as desired; keep surface covered with plastic wrap. With small spatula or decorating bags with small writing tips, decorate cookies with frosting (add warm water if you want a thinner consistency).

EACH TABLESPOON: ABOUT 40 CALORIES, 0G PROTEIN, 10G CARBOHYDRATE, 0G TOTAL FAT, 0G FIBER, 0MG CHOLESTEROL, 3MG SODIUM.

TIP
You'll find meringue powder in the baking aisle at the supermarket.

Decorating Cookies

Fear Not—It's Easy!

HOW TO TINT FROSTING

Whether you pipe it or spread it, decorating with colored Ornamental Frosting (opposite) is a great way to dress up any holiday cookie.

- **Liquid Food Coloring** Add the color, one drop at a time, stirring after each addition, until you reach the desired color.
- **Paste Food Coloring** Use a toothpick to remove a tiny portion of the paste, then stir the coloring into the frosting. For a deeper color, continue to add coloring in very small amounts.

HOW TO APPLY FROSTING

There's no other time of year when a cookie is judged for its decoration. But don't let that throw you. Follow these three easy steps to create beautiful iced cookies like our Butter Cookie Cutouts (page 15) or Gingerbread Cutouts (page 16).

- **Step 1** Fit a small disposable pastry bag or plastic food storage bag with a #2 round metal tip and fill with stiff Ornamental Frosting (left). Using constant, steady pressure, pipe an outline of the area on the cookie that you want to fill in; let dry.
- **Step 2** Thin a portion of the frosting with a small amount of water until it is the consistency of thick paint, and place in a separate bag. Cut the corner of the bag to a ½-inch opening and squeeze the frosting into the outlined area. Spread evenly with a toothpick.
- **Step 3** Add colored sugar crystals and other decorations while the frosting is still wet. Or, let the frosting dry and decoratively pipe the cookies with more stiff frosting.

EASY **Snickerdoodles**

These soft butter cookies with crunchy cinnamon-sugar coating are the perfect choice to leave for Santa on Christmas Eve.

ACTIVE TIME: 25 MINUTES   **TOTAL TIME:** 50 MINUTES PLUS COOLING   **MAKES:** 5 DOZEN COOKIES

Basic Cookie Dough (page 14)

¼ cup granulated sugar

1½ teaspoons ground cinnamon

1 Preheat oven to 375°F.

2 Prepare Basic Cookie Dough.

3 In small bowl, combine sugar and cinnamon. Roll dough by scant tablespoonfuls into 1-inch balls; roll in cinnamon sugar to coat evenly. Place balls, 1 inch apart, on large ungreased cookie sheet.

4 Bake for 12 minutes or until set, lightly golden, and slightly crinkly on top. Cool on cookie sheet on wire rack for 1 minute. With wide metal spatula, transfer cookies to wire racks to cool completely. Repeat with remaining dough.

EACH COOKIE: ABOUT 63 CALORIES, 1G PROTEIN, 8G CARBOHYDRATE, 3G TOTAL FAT (2G SATURATED), 0G FIBER, 11MG CHOLESTEROL, 39MG SODIUM.

ONE DOUGH DOES IT

Cranberry-Orange
SPICE COOKIES

Have leftover pumpkin pie spice from Thanksgiving?
Put it to good use in these scrumptious cookies with
dried cranberries, crystallized ginger, and orange peel.

ACTIVE TIME: 40 MINUTES **TOTAL TIME:** 1 HOUR PLUS FREEZING AND COOLING
MAKES: 5 DOZEN COOKIES

Basic Cookie Dough (page 14)

½ cup dried cranberries, finely chopped

¼ cup crystallized ginger, finely chopped

2 teaspoons freshly grated orange peel

1 teaspoon pumpkin pie spice

3 tablespoons green sugar crystals

3 tablespoons red sugar crystals

1 Prepare Basic Cookie Dough. In step 2, stir in cranberries, ginger, orange peel, and pumpkin pie spice along with flour until well mixed. Divide dough in half.

2 On lightly floured surface, with hands, shape each half into a 10-inch-long log. Using hands or two clean rulers on sides, press each log into a 10-inch-long squared-off log. Wrap each log in plastic wrap and freeze until firm enough to slice, about 2 hours, or refrigerate overnight.

3 Preheat oven to 350°F. On 1 sheet of waxed paper, place green sugar. Unwrap 1 log and press sides in sugar to coat. Cut log into ¼-inch-thick slices. Place slices, 1 inch apart, on large ungreased cookie sheet. Bake for 14 to 16 minutes or until golden. Transfer cookies to wire racks to cool completely. Repeat with red sugar and second log.

EACH COOKIE: ABOUT 70 CALORIES, 1G PROTEIN, 9G CARBOHYDRATE, 3G TOTAL FAT (2G SATURATED), 0G FIBER, 12MG CHOLESTEROL, 50MG SODIUM.

TIP

Once the dough is firm, you can also slice and bake a portion of one log and freeze the extras for up to 3 months.

CHOCOLATE-DIPPED
Peppermint Sticks

Our combo of peppermint-flavored dough, white chocolate,
and crushed mint candies makes these delicate cookies
the perfect candidate for a cookie swap. For photo, see page 6.

ACTIVE TIME: 35 MINUTES   **TOTAL TIME:** 1 HOUR PLUS FREEZING, COOLING, AND CHILLING
MAKES: 5 DOZEN COOKIES

Basic Cookie Dough (page 14)

¼ teaspoon peppermint extract

Green and red paste food coloring

5 ounces white chocolate, melted

6 green or red starlight mints, crushed

1 Prepare Basic Cookie Dough. Divide dough
in half; transfer half to another bowl. Stir
peppermint extract into 1 portion of dough.
Divide peppermint dough in half; transfer half to
another bowl. Tint 1 portion green, the other red.

2 Preheat oven to 350°F. Line 9" by 9" metal
baking pan with plastic wrap, extending wrap
over sides of pan. Pat plain dough into pan.
Freeze for 10 minutes. Pat green dough over half
of plain dough; pat red dough over remaining
plain dough. Freeze for 10 minutes.

3 Lift dough from pan using plastic wrap; place
on cutting board. Cut dough into thirds so that
one-third is all red on top, one-third is all green
on top, and middle third is half red and half
green. Cut each third crosswise into ⅜-inch
strips. Twist strips and place, 1½ inches apart,
on large ungreased cookie sheet. Bake for 11 to
13 minutes or until golden brown. With spatula,
transfer cookies to wire rack to cool completely.
Repeat with remaining dough.

4 Dip one end of each cooled cookie into melted
chocolate and place on waxed paper. Sprinkle
chocolate with crushed mints. Refrigerate
cookies 15 minutes or until chocolate sets.

EACH COOKIE: ABOUT 75 CALORIES, 1G PROTEIN,
9G CARBOHYDRATE, 4G TOTAL FAT (3G SATURATED),
0G FIBER, 13MG CHOLESTEROL, 50MG SODIUM.

TIP

To melt the chocolate, coarsely chop
and place in small microwave-safe bowl.
Microwave on medium (50% power) for
1 minute or until chocolate starts to melt,
stirring every 20 seconds. Remove from
microwave and stir until completely melted.

Stained Glass ORNAMENTS

To hang these from your Christmas tree, poke a small hole in each unbaked cookie with a skewer. After baking and cooling, thread a ribbon, string, or nylon fishing line through the hole.

ACTIVE TIME: 50 MINUTES   TOTAL TIME: 1 HOUR PLUS CHILLING AND COOLING
MAKES: 5 DOZEN COOKIES

Basic Cookie Dough (page 14)

1   bag (6.25 ounces) hard candy, such as sour balls

1 Prepare Basic Cookie Dough; divide into 3 pieces. Flatten each piece into a disk; wrap each in plastic wrap. Refrigerate for at least 2 hours or overnight, until dough is firm enough to roll.
2 While dough is chilling, place each color of hard candy in separate heavy-duty plastic bags. Place 1 bag on towel-covered work surface or floor. With meat mallet or rolling pin, lightly crush candy into small pieces about the size of coarsely chopped nuts, being careful not to crush until powdery. Repeat with remaining candy.

3 Preheat oven to 350°F. Line large cookie sheet with foil. Between two sheets of waxed paper, roll 1 disk of dough ⅛-inch thick. Remove top sheet of waxed paper. With 3- to 4-inch holiday-shaped cookie cutters, cut out as many cookies as possible. Place 1 inch apart on prepared cookie sheet. Cut out centers of cookies with 1½- to 2-inch holiday-shaped cookie cutters. Remove and refrigerate trimmings and cutout centers.
4 Bake for 7 minutes. Remove cookie sheet from oven; fill each cookie's center with ½ teaspoon crushed candy. Return to oven and bake for 3 to 4 minutes longer, or until cookies are lightly browned and candy is melted. Cool cookies completely on cookie sheet on wire rack. With metal spatula, remove cookies. Repeat with remaining dough, trimmings, and candy.

EACH COOKIE: ABOUT 70 CALORIES, 1G PROTEIN, 10G CARBOHYDRATE, 3G TOTAL FAT (2G SATURATED), 0G FIBER, 12MG CHOLESTEROL, 50MG SODIUM.

Chewy Fruit BARS

Chock full of dried dates, cherries, apricots, and raisins,
these easy bars may remind you of fruitcake—but without the fuss.

ACTIVE TIME: 20 MINUTES   TOTAL TIME: 45 MINUTES PLUS COOLING   MAKES: 4 DOZEN BARS

Basic Cookie Dough (page 14)

¾ teaspoon baking soda

1 teaspoon ground cinnamon

1½ cups packed dark brown sugar

2 large eggs

1 cup walnuts, chopped

1 cup pitted dried dates, chopped

1 cup dried tart cherries

½ cup dried apricot halves, chopped

½ cup golden raisins

Confectioners' sugar, optional

1 Preheat oven to 350°F. Line 15½" by 10½"
rimmed baking sheet with foil, extending over
rim; grease foil.

2 Prepare Basic Cookie Dough, but in step 1,
decrease flour to 2½ cups, increase baking soda
to ¾ teaspoon total, and add cinnamon to flour
mixture. In step 2, substitute 1½ cups packed
dark brown sugar for granulated sugar, and use
a total of 2 eggs. Add walnuts, dates, cherries,
apricots, and raisins to dough, stirring until
blended (dough will be thick).

3 With floured fingers, press dough evenly into
prepared pan. Bake for 25 to 28 minutes, or until
browned and toothpick inserted in center comes
out clean. Cool completely in pan on wire rack.
Using foil, remove bar from pan. With long, sharp
knife, cut lengthwise into 4 strips, then cut each
strip crosswise into 12 bars. Sift confectioners'
sugar over bars before serving, if desired.

EACH BAR: ABOUT 145 CALORIES, 2G PROTEIN,
23G CARBOHYDRATE, 6G TOTAL FAT (3G SATURATED),
1G FIBER, 24MG CHOLESTEROL, 70MG SODIUM.

CHOCOLATE
Pinwheels

Three kinds of chocolate—semisweet, unsweetened, and cocoa—
make these two-tone classics extra fudgy.

ACTIVE TIME: 30 MINUTES   **TOTAL TIME:** 50 MINUTES PLUS FREEZING AND COOLING
MAKES: 4 DOZEN COOKIES

Basic Cookie Dough (page 14)

⅓ cup miniature semisweet chocolate chips

¼ cup confectioners' sugar

1 ounce unsweetened chocolate, melted

2 tablespoons unsweetened cocoa powder

2 tablespoons all-purpose flour

1 Prepare Basic Cookie Dough. Divide dough in half; transfer half to another bowl. Stir chocolate chips, sugar, melted chocolate, and cocoa into half of dough. Stir flour into plain dough.

2 On sheet of waxed paper, roll chocolate dough into 14" by 10" rectangle. Repeat with plain dough. Turn over plain rectangle, still on waxed paper, and place, dough side down, on top of chocolate rectangle so that the edges line up evenly. Peel off top sheet of waxed paper. If dough becomes too soft to work with, refrigerate for 10 minutes. Starting from long side, tightly roll rectangles together, jelly-roll fashion, to form a log, lifting bottom sheet of waxed paper to help roll. Cut log crosswise in half. Wrap each half in plastic wrap and freeze for 2 hours or refrigerate overnight until dough is firm enough to slice.

3 Preheat oven to 350°F. With sharp knife, cut 1 log (keep other log refrigerated) into ¼-inch-thick slices. Place slices, about 2 inches apart, on large ungreased cookie sheet.

4 Bake cookies for 10 to 12 minutes or until lightly browned. Transfer cookies to wire racks to cool completely. Repeat with remaining log.

EACH COOKIE: ABOUT 90 CALORIES, 1G PROTEIN, 10G CARBOHYDRATE, 5G TOTAL FAT (3G SATURATED), 0G FIBER, 16MG CHOLESTEROL, 60MG SODIUM.

TIP

If the waxed paper wrinkles when rolling out the dough in step 2, peel off the paper and replace it before continuing.

Cranberry-Chocolate Chunk
Cookies (page 41)

2 Easy Drops

With only a spoon required to shape and bake, drop cookies are truly a hectic holiday baker's best friend. We have classic drops, like chewy Chocolate Chip Jumbos and Ginger Cookies. We also offer dressy yet super-easy drops, like our Christmas Fruit Drops and Cranberry-Pistachio Lace Cookies—both drizzled with white chocolate.

For even baking, keeping the size of drop cookies uniform and using the right kind of spoon makes all the difference. Most of our recipes use a measuring teaspoon or tablespoon with a level amount of dough ("rounded" spoonfuls are 1½ times the level measure of dough). Unless the recipe directs otherwise, place spoonfuls of dough 2 inches apart on the prepared cookie sheet.

Christmas Fruit
DROPS

Studded with walnuts and candied cherries, then drizzled with melted white chocolate, these buttery morsels are the ultimate holiday cookie jar treat.

ACTIVE TIME: 20 MINUTES **TOTAL TIME:** 1 HOUR PLUS STANDING **MAKES:** 6 DOZEN COOKIES

2½ cups all-purpose flour

1 teaspoon baking soda

½ teaspoon salt

1 cup (2 sticks) butter or margarine, softened

¾ cup granulated sugar

½ cup packed dark brown sugar

1 teaspoon vanilla extract

3 large eggs

2 cups toasted rice cereal

1 cup walnuts, toasted and coarsely chopped

½ cup red candied cherries, coarsely chopped

½ cup green candied cherries, coarsely chopped

1½ cups white chocolate chips

1 Preheat oven to 350°F. Grease large cookie sheet.

2 In medium bowl with wire whisk, combine flour, baking soda, and salt. In large bowl with mixer at medium speed, beat butter and sugars until light and fluffy, occasionally scraping bowl with rubber spatula. Beat in vanilla, then eggs, one at a time. Reduce speed to low; gradually beat in flour mixture just until blended, occasionally scraping bowl. With spoon, stir in cereal, walnuts, cherries, and 1 cup chocolate chips.

3 Drop dough by rounded teaspoons, 1 inch apart, on prepared cookie sheet. Bake for 10 to 11 minutes or until golden. With spatula, transfer cookies to wire racks to cool completely. Repeat with remaining dough.

4 Place remaining ½ cup chocolate chips in small microwave-safe bowl; microwave on medium (50% power) for about 2 minutes or until chocolate melts, stirring once. Stir until smooth. Place cookies on waxed paper; drizzle with melted chocolate. Let stand until chocolate sets.

EACH COOKIE: ABOUT 100 CALORIES, 1G PROTEIN, 12G CARBOHYDRATE, 6G TOTAL FAT (2G SATURATED), 0G FIBER, 17MG CHOLESTEROL, 80MG SODIUM.

TIP

To chop the candied cherries, spray your knife with nonstick cooking spray so the fruit doesn't stick.

Butter Up!

Rookie cookie bakers: take note of these must-have tips.

You've probably noticed that many of our recipes, like Holiday Oatmeal Cookies (page 43) and Peanut Butter Cookies (page 33), call for softened butter. That's no accident. Softened butter mixes far more easily with sugar and flour than hard, cold butter. And unlike room-temperature butter, it should still hold its shape but dent when pressed. There are two ways to soften butter quickly:

- **Pound It.** Place wrapped stick of butter between two pieces of parchment or waxed paper. With rolling pin, pound the stick several times on each side to partially flatten.
- **Beat It.** Cut cold butter into small chunks. With mixer at medium-high speed, beat it solo until softened, occasionally scraping bowl with rubber spatula, before adding additional ingredients.

No portion of softened butter should be melted (as it can vastly effect the texture of baked cookies), so avoid using the microwave. Margarine is already soft straight from the fridge, so you don't need to soften before using it in a recipe.

Peanut Butter COOKIES

Kids of all ages, not to mention Santa, will love these
chewy classics with a glass of ice-cold milk.

ACTIVE TIME: 40 MINUTES   **TOTAL TIME:** 1 HOUR 15 MINUTES PLUS COOLING
MAKES: ABOUT 6 DOZEN COOKIES

2 cups all-purpose flour

1 teaspoon baking powder

1 teaspoon baking soda

1 teaspoon salt

1 cup (2 sticks) butter, softened

1 cup packed brown sugar

1 cup plus 2 tablespoons granulated sugar

1 teaspoon vanilla extract

2 large eggs

1 jar (18 ounces) creamy peanut butter

1 Preheat oven to 350°F. In medium bowl with
wire whisk, combine flour, baking powder,
baking soda, and salt.

2 In large bowl with mixer on medium speed,
beat butter, brown sugar, and 1 cup granulated
sugar for 2 minutes or until light and fluffy,
occasionally scraping bowl with rubber spatula.
Reduce speed to low; beat in vanilla and then
eggs, one at a time, beating well after each
addition. Add peanut butter, increase speed to
medium, and beat for 2 minutes or until creamy.

Reduce speed to low; gradually beat in flour
mixture just until blended, occasionally scraping
bowl.

3 Drop dough by rounded measuring
tablespoons, 2 inches apart, on large ungreased
cookie sheet. Place remaining 2 tablespoons
granulated sugar on plate or sheet of waxed
paper. Dip tines of fork in sugar, then press twice
into top of each cookie, making a crisscross
pattern.

4 Bake for 12 to 14 minutes or until lightly
browned at edges. Cool cookies on cookie sheet
for 2 minutes. With spatula, transfer cookies
to wire racks to cool completely. Repeat with
remaining dough and sugar.

EACH COOKIE: ABOUT 105 CALORIES, 2G PROTEIN,
10G CARBOHYDRATE, 7G TOTAL FAT (3G SATURATED),
1G FIBER, 13MG CHOLESTEROL, 120MG SODIUM.

TIP

If storing soft cookies (like these) at room
temperature, add a wedge of apple or slice
of white bread to the container to keep
them moist. Replace the fruit or bread
every couple of days. Try it with our Ginger
Cookies (page 35), too.

Chocolate Chip
JUMBOS

When we say these cookies are jumbos, we mean it—
one is equivalent to six regular-size cookies. So be sure you share!

ACTIVE TIME: 40 MINUTES   **TOTAL TIME:** 1 HOUR 25 MINUTES PLUS COOLING
MAKES: ABOUT 3 DOZEN COOKIES

3   large eggs

1   pound (4 sticks) butter or margarine, softened

1   package (16 ounces) brown sugar

1½ cups granulated sugar

2   tablespoons vanilla extract

1½ teaspoons baking soda

1½ teaspoons salt

6   cups all-purpose flour

2   packages (12 ounces each) semisweet chocolate chips

1   bag (16 ounces) chopped walnuts

1 Arrange oven racks in top and bottom thirds of oven. Preheat oven to 350°F. Line two large cookie sheets with parchment paper.

2 In very large bowl with mixer on medium speed, beat eggs for 4 minutes or until light and fluffy. Reduce speed to low; beat in butter, sugars, vanilla, baking soda, and salt. Stir in flour, chocolate chips, and walnuts (mixture will be very stiff).

3 Drop dough by level ⅓ cups (or use 2½-inch ice cream scoop) 2 inches apart on prepared cookie sheets. Bake for 23 to 26 minutes or until golden around the edges, rotating cookie sheets between upper and lower racks halfway through baking. With spatula, transfer cookies to wire racks to cool completely. Repeat with remaining dough, reusing the same parchment.

EACH COOKIE: ABOUT 425 CALORIES, 6G PROTEIN, 50G CARBOHYDRATE, 25G TOTAL FAT (11G SATURATED), 3G FIBER, 45MG CHOLESTEROL, 265MG SODIUM.

Ginger COOKIES

These spicy cookies are particularly delicious when served with mulled cider.

ACTIVE TIME: 20 MINUTES   **TOTAL TIME:** 30 MINUTES PLUS COOLING   **MAKES:** ABOUT 30 COOKIES

2   cups all-purpose flour

2   teaspoons ground ginger

1   teaspoon baking soda

½   teaspoon ground cinnamon

½   teaspoon salt

¼   teaspoon ground black pepper, optional

¾   cup vegetable shortening

½   cup plus 2 tablespoons sugar

1   large egg

½   cup dark molasses

1 Arrange oven racks in upper and lower thirds of oven. Preheat oven to 350°F.

2 In medium bowl with wire whisk, combine flour, ginger, baking soda, cinnamon, salt, and pepper, if desired.

3 In large bowl with mixer on medium speed, beat shortening and ½ cup sugar until light and fluffy. Beat in egg until blended; beat in molasses, occasionally scraping bowl with rubber spatula.

Reduce speed to low; gradually beat in flour mixture just until blended, occasionally scraping bowl.

4 Place remaining 2 tablespoons sugar on sheet of waxed paper. Roll dough by slightly rounded tablespoonfuls into balls; roll in sugar to coat evenly. Place balls, 2 inches apart, on two large ungreased cookie sheets. Bake for 9 to 11 minutes or until set, rotating cookie sheets between upper and lower racks halfway through baking. Cookies will be very soft and may appear moist in cracks. Cool for 1 minute on cookie sheets on wire racks; with metal spatula, transfer cookies to wire racks to cool completely.

EACH COOKIE: ABOUT 107 CALORIES, 1G PROTEIN, 14G CARBOHYDRATE, 6G TOTAL FAT (1G SATURATED), 0G FIBER, 7MG CHOLESTEROL, 86MG SODIUM.

 TIP

You can also make jumbo gingersnaps! Prepare the recipe as directed but in step 4, roll dough by ½ cupfuls, place 4 inches apart on cookie sheets, and bake about 15 minutes. Makes 10 giant cookies.

Chocolate PB DROPS

Kids of all ages will love these old-fashioned butter cookies
with a chocolate-and-peanut butter drizzle.

ACTIVE TIME: 30 MINUTES   **TOTAL TIME:** 1 HOUR PLUS COOLING AND CHILLING
MAKES: ABOUT 3½ DOZEN COOKIES

2¼ cups all-purpose flour

1   teaspoon baking powder

½   teaspoon baking soda

¾   cup (1½ sticks) butter, softened

¾   cup granulated sugar

½   teaspoon salt

1   large egg yolk

2   tablespoons light corn syrup

1½ teaspoons vanilla extract

3   tablespoons peanut butter

2   ounces bittersweet chocolate, melted

1 Preheat oven to 375°F. Line large cookie sheet
with parchment paper.

2 In medium bowl with wire whisk, combine
flour, baking powder, and baking soda.

3 In large bowl with mixer on medium-high
speed, beat butter, sugar, and salt until light and
fluffy. Beat in egg yolk, corn syrup, and vanilla
until smooth, occasionally scraping bowl with
rubber spatula. Reduce speed to medium-low;
gradually beat in flour mixture just until blended,
occasionally scraping bowl.

4 With 1-tablespoon measuring spoon, form
dough into balls. Place balls, 1 inch apart, on
prepared cookie sheet. Flatten tops lightly. Bake
for 15 minutes or until golden.

5 Slide cookies, still on parchment, onto wire
rack to cool completely. Repeat with remaining
dough and cooled, newly lined cookie sheet.

6 Place peanut butter in small microwave-safe
bowl; microwave on high for 40 to 60 seconds,
stirring every 20 seconds, or until hot. When
cookies have cooled, drizzle with melted chocolate
and peanut butter. Refrigerate for about 1½
hours, until chocolate and peanut butter set.

EACH COOKIE: ABOUT 86 CALORIES, 1G PROTEIN,
11G CARBOHYDRATE, 5G TOTAL FAT (3G SATURATED),
0G FIBER, 13MG CHOLESTEROL, 83MG SODIUM.

Cherry-Walnut DROPS

These extra-tender morsels, made with a butter and cream cheese dough, are studded with dried cherries and nuts.

ACTIVE TIME: 25 MINUTES   **TOTAL TIME:** 1 HOUR PLUS COOLING AND STANDING
MAKES: ABOUT 4 DOZEN COOKIES

1   cup (2 sticks) butter, softened

1   package (8 ounces) full-fat cream cheese, softened

1   cup granulated sugar

½   teaspoon salt

1   large egg yolk

1½ teaspoons vanilla extract

2½ cups all-purpose flour

1   cup dried cherries

1   cup walnuts, finely chopped

1   Preheat oven to 375°F.

2   In large bowl with mixer on medium-high speed, beat butter, cream cheese, sugar, and salt until light and fluffy. Beat in egg yolk and vanilla, occasionally scraping bowl with rubber spatula. Reduce speed to low; gradually beat in flour just until blended, occasionally scraping bowl. Stir in cherries and nuts.

3   With 1-tablespoon measuring spoon, form dough into balls. Place balls, 2 inches apart, onto large ungreased cookie sheet. Bake for 12 to 18 minutes or until deep golden brown around edges. Cool cookies on cookie sheet on wire rack for 10 minutes. With spatula, transfer cookies to wire racks to cool completely. Repeat with remaining dough.

EACH COOKIE: ABOUT 116 CALORIES, 2G PROTEIN, 12G CARBOHYDRATE, 7G TOTAL FAT (4G SATURATED), 1G FIBER, 19MG CHOLESTEROL, 69MG SODIUM.

Left: Cranberry-Pistachio Lace Cookies (opposite); right: Chocolate-Coconut Lace Cookies (page 40)

Cranberry-Pistachio
LACE COOKIES

These ultra-thin, crunchy cookies get their lacy texture
from melted butter and light corn syrup.

ACTIVE TIME: 20 MINUTES　　**TOTAL TIME:** 40 MINUTES PLUS COOLING　　**MAKES:** ABOUT 6 DOZEN COOKIES

- ½ cup old-fashioned oats, uncooked
- ½ cup shelled pistachios
- ⅓ cup dried cranberries
- ½ cup all-purpose flour
- ½ cup granulated sugar
- ¼ teaspoon ground cinnamon
- ¼ teaspoon baking powder

Pinch salt

- ½ cup (1 stick) butter or margarine, melted
- 2 tablespoons heavy or whipping cream
- 2 tablespoons light corn syrup
- 1 teaspoon vanilla extract
- 2 ounces white chocolate, melted (optional)

1 Arrange oven racks in top and bottom thirds of oven. Preheat oven to 375°F. Line two large cookie sheets with parchment paper.

2 In food processor with knife blade attached, pulse oats and pistachios just until finely chopped. Transfer to large bowl. To food processor bowl, add cranberries. Pulse until finely chopped; set aside.

3 To bowl with oats, add flour, sugar, cinnamon, baking powder, and salt; whisk to combine.

4 In large bowl with mixer on low speed, beat butter, cream, corn syrup, and vanilla until well combined. In batches, add flour mixture to butter mixture, beating well between additions. Stir in cranberries.

5 Using measuring teaspoon, drop batter by level spoonfuls, 3 inches apart, on prepared cookie sheet. Bake for 7 to 8 minutes or until golden brown, rotating cookie sheets between upper and lower racks halfway through baking. Slide cookies, still on parchment, onto wire racks to cool completely. Repeat with remaining dough and cooled, newly lined cookie sheets.

6 Drizzle cooled cookies with melted chocolate, if desired. Refrigerate for about 15 minutes or until chocolate sets.

EACH COOKIE: ABOUT 30 CALORIES, 0G PROTEIN, 4G CARBOHYDRATE, 2G TOTAL FAT (1G SATURATED), 0G FIBER, 4MG CHOLESTEROL, 15MG SODIUM.

TIP

To make a picture-perfect drizzle in step 6, transfer the melted white chocolate to a small plastic bag, cut a tiny hole in the corner, and pipe chocolate onto cookies.

Chocolate-Coconut
LACE COOKIES

Chopped roasted cashews and a touch of heavy cream make these special-occasion cookies extra indulgent. For photo, see page 38.

ACTIVE TIME: 20 MINUTES   **TOTAL TIME:** 40 MINUTES PLUS COOLING   **MAKES:** ABOUT 6 DOZEN COOKIES

½ cup old-fashioned oats, uncooked

½ cup roasted unsalted cashews

½ cup sweetened shredded coconut

½ cup all-purpose flour

½ cup granulated sugar

¼ teaspoon ground cinnamon

¼ teaspoon baking powder

Pinch salt

½ cup (1 stick) butter or margarine, melted

2 tablespoons heavy or whipping cream

2 tablespoons light corn syrup

1 teaspoon vanilla extract

2 ounces dark chocolate, melted (optional)

1 Arrange oven racks in top and bottom thirds of oven. Preheat oven to 375°F. Line two large cookie sheets with parchment paper.

2 In food processor with knife blade attached, pulse oats and cashews just until finely chopped. Transfer to large bowl. To food processor bowl, add coconut. Pulse until finely chopped; set aside.

3 To bowl with oats, add flour, sugar, cinnamon, baking powder, and salt; whisk to combine.

4 In large bowl with mixer on low speed, beat butter, cream, corn syrup, and vanilla until well combined. In batches, add flour mixture to butter mixture, beating well between additions.

5 Using measuring teaspoon, drop batter by level spoonfuls, 3 inches apart, on prepared cookie sheets. Bake for 7 to 8 minutes or until golden brown, rotating cookie sheets between upper and lower racks halfway through baking. Slide cookies, still on parchment, onto wire racks to cool completely. Repeat with remaining dough and cooled, newly lined cookie sheets.

6 With pastry brush, brush half of each cookie top with melted chocolate, if desired. Refrigerate for about 15 minutes or until chocolate sets.

EACH COOKIE: ABOUT 40 CALORIES, 0G PROTEIN, 4G CARBOHYDRATE, 2G TOTAL FAT (1G SATURATED), 0G FIBER, 4MG CHOLESTEROL, 18MG SODIUM.

Cranberry-Chocolate
CHUNK COOKIES

Dried cranberries and two kinds of chocolate give these cookie jar treats their holiday spin. For photo, see page 28.

ACTIVE TIME: 30 MINUTES   **TOTAL TIME:** 1 HOUR PLUS CHILLING AND COOLING   **MAKES:** 3 DOZEN COOKIES

2½ cups all-purpose flour

1   teaspoon baking soda

½   teaspoon salt

¾   cup (1½ sticks) butter or margarine, softened

¾   cup packed dark brown sugar

¼   cup granulated sugar

3   tablespoons light corn syrup

2   large eggs

2   teaspoons vanilla extract

1¼ cups walnuts, toasted and chopped

1   cup dried cranberries

4   ounces white chocolate, chopped

4   ounces semisweet chocolate, chopped

1 Arrange oven racks in upper and lower thirds of oven. Preheat oven to 375°F. Line three cookie sheets with parchment paper.

2 In medium bowl with wire whisk, combine flour, baking soda, and salt. In large bowl with mixer on medium speed, beat butter, sugars, and corn syrup just until creamy. Beat in eggs and vanilla until blended. Reduce speed to low. In two batches, add flour mixture, beating between batches just until blended. Stir in two-thirds of walnuts, cranberries, and chocolate pieces. Refrigerate dough for 15 minutes or up to 1 day.

3 Drop dough by rounded tablespoons, 2 inches apart, on prepared cookie sheets (return remaining dough to refrigerator for next batch). Bake for 5 minutes. Working quickly, press some of remaining nuts, cranberries, and chocolate pieces into cookies. Rotate sheets on racks; bake for 6 to 8 minutes more or until edges are golden brown.

4 With spatula, transfer cookies to wire racks to cool completely. Repeat with remaining dough and cooled, newly lined cookie sheets.

EACH COOKIE: ABOUT 170 CALORIES, 2G PROTEIN, 21G CARBOHYDRATE, 9G TOTAL FAT (4G SATURATED), 1G FIBER, 21MG CHOLESTEROL, 75MG SODIUM.

HOLIDAY
Oatmeal Cookies

Make this soft and chewy classic even better
by using plenty of raisins and adding chocolate chips.

ACTIVE TIME: 40 MINUTES   **TOTAL TIME:** 1 HOUR 10 MINUTES PLUS COOLING
MAKES: ABOUT 4 DOZEN COOKIES

1½ cups all-purpose flour

1   teaspoon baking soda

½   teaspoon salt

1   cup (2 sticks) butter or margarine, softened

¾   cup packed brown sugar

½   cup granulated sugar

1   large egg

1   teaspoon vanilla extract

3   cups old-fashioned oats, uncooked

1   cup raisins

1   cup semisweet chocolate chips

1 Preheat oven to 350°F. In medium bowl with wire whisk, combine flour, baking soda, and salt.
2 In large bowl with mixer on medium speed, beat butter and sugars until light and fluffy, occasionally scraping bowl with rubber spatula. Beat in egg and vanilla. Reduce speed to low; gradually beat in flour mixture just until blended, occasionally scraping bowl. With spoon, stir in oats, raisins, and chocolate chips.
3 Drop dough by heaping measuring tablespoons, 2 inches apart, on large ungreased cookie sheet. Bake for 13 to 15 minutes or until tops are golden. With spatula, transfer cookies to wire racks to cool completely. Repeat with remaining dough.

EACH COOKIE: ABOUT 115 CALORIES, 2G PROTEIN, 16G CARBOHYDRATE, 6G TOTAL FAT (3G SATURATED), 1G FIBER, 15MG CHOLESTEROL, 95MG SODIUM.

TIP

Always cool cookie sheets between batches. Placing dough on hot metal will make the batter spread before it's in the oven, causing the cookies to be too flat.

Spice DROPS

Coarse sugar crystals give these gently spiced cookies a sparkling appearance and wonderful crunch.

ACTIVE TIME: 25 MINUTES   **TOTAL TIME:** 55 MINUTES PLUS COOLING   **MAKES:** ABOUT 3½ DOZEN COOKIES

2¼ cups all-purpose flour

2½ teaspoons ground cinnamon

2 teaspoons ground ginger

¼ teaspoon ground cloves

1 teaspoon baking powder

½ teaspoon baking soda

¾ cup (1½ sticks) butter, softened

¾ cup granulated sugar

½ teaspoon salt

1 large egg yolk

2 tablespoons light corn syrup

1½ teaspoons vanilla extract

¼ cup coarse white sugar crystals

1 Preheat oven to 375°F. Line large cookie sheet with parchment paper.

2 In medium bowl with wire whisk, combine flour, cinnamon, ginger, cloves, baking powder, and baking soda.

3 In large bowl with mixer on medium-high speed, beat butter, sugar, and salt until light and fluffy. Beat in egg yolk, corn syrup, and vanilla until smooth, occasionally scraping bowl with rubber spatula. Reduce speed to medium-low; gradually beat in flour mixture just until blended, occasionally scraping bowl.

4 With 1-tablespoon measuring spoon, form dough into balls; roll in coarse sugar. Place balls, 1 inch apart, on prepared cookie sheet. Flatten tops lightly. Bake for 15 minutes or until edges are set.

5 Slide cookies, still on parchment, onto wire rack to cool completely. Repeat with remaining dough and cooled, newly lined cookie sheet.

EACH COOKIE: ABOUT 77 CALORIES, 1G PROTEIN, 11G CARBOHYDRATE, 4G TOTAL FAT (2G SATURATED), 0G FIBER, 13MG CHOLESTEROL, 79MG SODIUM.

Chocolate-Filled Biscotti (page 50)
and English Tea Cakes (page 63)

3 Holiday Heirlooms

Many of the most beloved holiday cookies hail from other countries, passed from one generation to the next. This cookie sampler includes favorites like Italian biscotti (we offer three scrumptious varieties), plus Lebkuchen and Spritz Cookies from Germany. We also put our personal stamp on several old-world classics, like Best Linzer Cookies, English Tea Cakes, and Salted Toffee Rugelach.

These recipes offer the perfect opportunity to assemble a *mise en place*, the French term for a lineup of premeasured ingredients, on the counter before you begin. This reduces your chances of omitting an ingredient or measuring incorrectly. Now that's a smart tradition to adopt for any cookie!

CHRISTMAS
Macarons

French Macarons are a meringue-based cookie made with ground almonds and then filled with buttercream, chocolate ganache, or fruit curd. Our simplified version uses melted bittersweet chocolate.

ACTIVE TIME: 25 MINUTES   **TOTAL TIME:** 1 HOUR PLUS COOLING AND STANDING
MAKES: 3 DOZEN COOKIES

1 cup slivered almonds

2 cups lightly packed confectioners' sugar

3 large egg whites, at room temperature

¼ teaspoon salt

7 drops green liquid food coloring

¼ teaspoon almond extract

4 ounces bittersweet chocolate, melted

1 Preheat oven to 300°F. Line two large cookie sheets with parchment paper.

2 In food processor with knife blade attached, process almonds and 1 cup sugar until finely ground and powdery, occasionally scraping bowl with rubber spatula. Add remaining sugar; pulse until combined. Transfer to large bowl.

3 In large bowl with mixer on medium speed, beat egg whites and salt until soft peaks form. Beat in food coloring and almond extract. Increase speed to high and beat just until stiff (but not dry) peaks form when beaters are lifted. With rubber spatula, fold egg whites into almond mixture until blended. Batter will be just pourable and sticky.

4 Transfer batter to pastry bag fitted with ½-inch round tip. Holding bag about ½ inch above parchment, pipe 1-inch rounds spaced 1½ inches apart (batter will spread). Let stand for 20 minutes.

5 Bake, one cookie sheet at a time, for 18 to 19 minutes or until bubbles around bases of macarons are firm to the touch but tops are not browned. Slide cookies, still on parchment, onto wire rack to cool completely. Repeat with second cookie sheet.

6 When cookies are cool, spread melted chocolate on bottoms of half of macarons, using about ½ teaspoon for each. Top each with another macaron, bottom side down. Let stand until chocolate hardens, about 45 minutes.

EACH COOKIE: ABOUT 60 CALORIES, 1G PROTEIN, 9G CARBOHYDRATE, 3G TOTAL FAT (1G SATURATED), 1G FIBER, 0MG CHOLESTEROL, 20MG SODIUM.

Chocolate-Filled
BISCOTTI

Food Director Susan Westmoreland bakes these cookies for her great aunt Mary every Christmas. The cookies bake only once, not twice, so they're chocolaty and chewy (not hard like most biscotti). For photo, see page 46.

ACTIVE TIME: 30 MINUTES   **TOTAL TIME:** 1 HOUR PLUS CHILLING AND COOLING   **MAKES:** 8 DOZEN COOKIES

CREAM CHEESE DOUGH

4   cups all-purpose flour

1   teaspoon baking powder

1   teaspoon salt

1   cup (2 sticks) butter, softened

6   ounces cream cheese, softened

1   cup granulated sugar

1   cup packed brown sugar

2   large eggs

1   tablespoon vanilla extract

CHOCOLATE FILLING

1   can (14 ounces) sweetened condensed milk

8   ounces bittersweet or semisweet chocolate, cut up

1   cup walnuts, coarsely chopped

Confectioners' sugar

1 Prepare Cream Cheese Dough: In medium bowl with wire whisk, combine flour, baking powder, and salt.

2 In large bowl with mixer on medium speed, beat butter and cream cheese until well blended. Gradually add sugars and beat for 3 minutes or until light and fluffy, occasionally scraping bowl with rubber spatula. Add eggs, one at a time, beating well after each addition. Beat in vanilla. Reduce speed to low; gradually beat in flour mixture just until blended, occasionally scraping bowl.

3 Place level ¾ cup dough on sheet of plastic wrap. Repeat to make seven more ¾-cupfuls. Wrap each with plastic wrap and refrigerate overnight.

4 Prepare Chocolate Filling: When ready to roll out dough, in 2-quart saucepan, heat sweetened condensed milk and chocolate over medium heat just until chocolate melts, stirring frequently. Remove saucepan from heat; stir in walnuts. Cool filling to room temperature, about 30 minutes.

5 Preheat oven to 350°F. Grease two large cookie sheets.

6 Remove 1 piece of dough from refrigerator. On lightly floured 16-inch sheet of waxed paper, with floured rolling pin, roll dough into 10" by 6" rectangle. Spread heaping ¼ cup filling lengthwise down center of rectangle. Starting from a long side and using waxed paper to help lift dough, fold one side of dough lengthwise over filling, then remaining side over dough (dough should overlap).

7 Pick up waxed paper and flip cookie log onto one side of prepared cookie sheet, seam side down. Repeat with another piece of dough and filling. Flip second log parallel to first log, leaving about 2 inches between logs.

8 Bake for 20 to 22 minutes or until edges are lightly golden. Cool on cookie sheet for 2 minutes. With spatula, transfer logs to wire rack to cool completely.

9 While logs bake, repeat with remaining dough and filling. To serve, sift confectioners' sugar over cooled logs. Cut each log crosswise on the diagonal into 12 slices.

EACH COOKIE: ABOUT 95 CALORIES, 2G PROTEIN, 12G CARBOHYDRATE, 5G TOTAL FAT (3G SATURATED), 0G FIBER, 13MG CHOLESTEROL, 60MG SODIUM.

Walnut BISCOTTI

Biscotti (which means "baked twice") are crisp cookies that can be dunked in espresso or sweet wine to enjoy as a dessert or snack.

ACTIVE TIME: 40 MINUTES TOTAL TIME: 1 HOUR 40 MINUTES PLUS COOLING
MAKES: ABOUT 3 DOZEN COOKIES

2 cups all-purpose flour

1½ teaspoons baking powder

¼ teaspoon salt

½ cup (1 stick) butter, softened

⅓ cup granulated sugar

⅓ cup packed brown sugar

2 large eggs

1 tablespoon vanilla extract

1 cup walnuts, toasted and chopped

12 ounces white chocolate, melted (optional)

1 Preheat oven to 325°F. Line large cookie sheet with parchment paper.

2 In medium bowl with wire whisk, combine flour, baking powder, and salt.

3 In large bowl with mixer on medium speed, beat butter and sugars until light and fluffy. Add eggs, one at a time, beating well after each addition. Beat in vanilla. Reduce speed to low; gradually beat in flour mixture just until blended, occasionally scraping bowl with rubber spatula. Stir in walnuts.

4 Divide dough in half. Form each half into a 1½-inch-wide log on prepared cookie sheet, about 3 inches apart. Bake for 30 minutes or until golden brown. Cool on cookie sheet on wire rack for 5 minutes.

5 Slide logs onto cutting board. With serrated knife, cut each log crosswise into ½-inch-thick diagonal slices; place cut side down on same sheet. Bake for 20 to 25 minutes or until golden brown and crisp. Cool completely on cookie sheet on wire rack.

6 Dip half of each cooled cookie into melted chocolate, if desired; place on waxed paper. Let stand until chocolate sets.

EACH COOKIE: ABOUT 90 CALORIES, 2G PROTEIN, 10G CARBOHYDRATE, 5G TOTAL FAT (2G SATURATED), 0G FIBER, 17MG CHOLESTEROL, 45MG SODIUM.

Chocolate Brownie
BISCOTTI

Chocoholics will love this crisp rendition
of their all-time favorite bar cookie.

ACTIVE TIME: 45 MINUTES   **TOTAL TIME:** 1 HOUR 35 MINUTES PLUS COOLING
MAKES: ABOUT 3 DOZEN COOKIES

2½ cups all-purpose flour

1⅓ cups granulated sugar

¾ cup unsweetened cocoa

2 teaspoons baking powder

½ teaspoon baking soda

½ teaspoon salt

½ cup (1 stick) butter or margarine, melted

3 large eggs

2 teaspoons vanilla extract

1 cup almonds, toasted and coarsely chopped

4 ounces semisweet chocolate, coarsely chopped

1 Preheat oven to 325°F. In medium bowl with wire whisk, combine flour, sugar, cocoa, baking powder, baking soda, and salt.

2 In large bowl with mixer at medium speed, beat butter, eggs, and vanilla until mixed. Reduce speed to low; gradually add flour mixture and beat just until blended. By hand, knead in almonds and chocolate until combined.

3 Divide dough in half. On large ungreased cookie sheet, shape each half into 12" by 3" log, about 3 inches apart. Bake for 30 minutes. Cool logs on cookie sheet on wire rack for 15 minutes.

4 Place logs on cutting board. With serrated knife, cut each log crosswise into ½-inch-thick diagonal slices. With long metal spatula, place slices, top side up, ¼ inch apart, on same cookie sheet. Bake slices for 20 minutes to allow biscotti to dry out. Cool biscotti completely on cookie sheet on wire rack. (Biscotti will harden as they cool.)

EACH COOKIE: ABOUT 135 CALORIES, 3G PROTEIN, 17G CARBOHYDRATE, 7G TOTAL FAT (3G SATURATED), 2G FIBER, 25MG CHOLESTEROL, 105MG SODIUM.

Lemony Ricotta PILLOWS

Ricotta cheese makes these Italian-style cookies extra tender.
Be sure to use full-fat ricotta for best results.

ACTIVE TIME: 30 MINUTES **TOTAL TIME:** 1 HOUR PLUS COOLING AND STANDING
MAKES: ABOUT 3½ DOZEN COOKIES

- 1   lemon
- 4   cups all-purpose flour
- 2   teaspoons baking powder
- 1   teaspoon salt
- 1¾ cups granulated sugar
- 1   cup (2 sticks) butter, softened
- 1   container (15 ounces) ricotta cheese
- 2   large eggs
- 2   teaspoons vanilla extract
- 1¼ cups confectioners' sugar
- Blue food coloring
- Silver Stars Edible Accents
     (available at wilton.com), optional

1   Preheat oven to 350°F. From lemon, grate
1 teaspoon peel and squeeze 3 tablespoons
juice. In large bowl with wire whisk, combine
flour, baking powder, and salt. In another large
bowl with mixer on medium-high speed, beat
granulated sugar, butter, and lemon peel until
light and fluffy. Add ricotta, eggs, and vanilla,
beating until combined, occasionally scraping
bowl with rubber spatula. Reduce speed to low;
gradually beat in flour mixture just until blended,
occasionally scraping bowl.

2   Line large cookie sheet with parchment paper.
With small cookie scoop (about 2 teaspoons),
scoop dough into balls; place balls, 1½ inches
apart, on cookie sheet. With fingers, pat each
down into flat disk. Bake for 15 to 20 minutes or
until bottoms are golden brown. Cool cookies on
cookie sheet for 5 minutes. Slide cookies, still on
parchment, onto wire racks to cool completely.
Repeat with remaining dough and cooled, newly
lined cookie sheets.

3   **Prepare glaze:** In medium bowl, stir
confectioners' sugar, reserved lemon juice, and
½ teaspoon water until smooth. Tint with food
coloring to desired shade. Place in small plastic
bag with one corner snipped off and drizzle all
over cookies. Decorate with Silver Stars Edible
Accents, if desired. Let stand until glaze sets,
about 30 minutes.

EACH COOKIE: ABOUT 150 CALORIES, 3G PROTEIN,
22G CARBOHYDRATE, 6G TOTAL FAT (4G SATURATED),
0G FIBER, 26MG CHOLESTEROL, 130MG SODIUM.

Chocolate-Glazed RICOTTA COOKIES

Proceed with the recipe as directed but omit
lemon peel and juice in step 1. Substitute **6 ounces
melted dark chocolate** for the glaze in step 3.

EACH COOKIE: ABOUT 175 CALORIES, 3G PROTEIN,
23G CARBOHYDRATE, 8G TOTAL FAT (5G SATURATED),
1G FIBER, 26MG CHOLESTEROL, 121MG SODIUM.

Mostaccioli COOKIES

These chocolate spice cookies topped with a chocolate glaze
are an Italian holiday tradition.

ACTIVE TIME: 45 MINUTES   TOTAL TIME: 1 HOUR 15 MINUTES PLUS COOLING AND STANDING
MAKES: 5 DOZEN COOKIES

COOKIES

2   cups all-purpose flour

½   cup unsweetened cocoa

1½ teaspoons baking powder

1   teaspoon ground cinnamon

¼   teaspoon ground cloves

¼   teaspoon salt

½   cup (1 stick) butter or margarine, softened

¾   cup granulated sugar

1   large egg

½   cup whole milk

CHOCOLATE GLAZE

3   tablespoons unsweetened cocoa

1¼ cups confectioners' sugar

White candy decors, optional

1 Prepare Cookies: Preheat oven to 400°F. In medium bowl with wire whisk, combine flour, cocoa, baking powder, cinnamon, cloves, and salt. In large bowl with mixer at low speed, beat butter and granulated sugar until mixed, occasionally scraping bowl with rubber spatula. Increase speed to high; beat until light and fluffy. Reduce speed to low; beat in egg. Alternately add flour mixture and milk, beginning and ending with flour mixture, just until combined, occasionally scraping bowl.

2 With cocoa-dusted hands, shape dough by level tablespoons into 1-inch balls. Place balls, 2 inches apart, on large ungreased cookie sheet. Bake for 7 to 9 minutes or until puffed (cookies will look dry and slightly cracked). With spatula, transfer cookies to wire rack to cool completely. Repeat with remaining dough.

3 Prepare Chocolate Glaze: When cookies are cool, in medium bowl, with wire whisk or fork, gradually mix cocoa with *¼ cup boiling water* until smooth. Gradually stir in confectioners' sugar and blend well. Dip top of each cookie into glaze. Place cookies on wire rack set over waxed paper to catch any drips. Immediately sprinkle cookies with decors, if desired. Let stand until glaze sets, about 20 minutes.

EACH COOKIE: ABOUT 55 CALORIES, 1G PROTEIN, 9G CARBOHYDRATE, 2G TOTAL FAT (1G SATURATED), 0.5G FIBER, 8MG CHOLESTEROL, 40MG SODIUM.

Pine Nut COOKIES

While these classic Italian cookies bake, the delicate flavor
of the pine nut (aka pignoli) coating deepens.

ACTIVE TIME: 40 MINUTES **TOTAL TIME:** 1 HOUR 10 MINUTES PLUS CHILLING AND COOLING
MAKES: ABOUT 2½ DOZEN COOKIES

2 large egg whites

1 tube (7 ounces) or 1 can (8 ounces) almond
paste, broken into pieces

½ cup confectioners' sugar

¼ cup granulated sugar

¼ cup all-purpose flour

Pinch salt

1¼ cups pine nuts (pignoli)

1 In large bowl with mixer at low speed, beat
egg whites until foamy. Add almond paste and
beat until crumbly. Increase speed to medium-
high; beat for about 2 minutes or until almost
smooth, occasionally scraping bowl with rubber
spatula (mixture will look grainy). Reduce
speed to medium; beat in sugar for 1 minute or
until creamy. Add flour and salt; beat just until
blended (dough will be sticky). Cover bowl with
plastic wrap and refrigerate for at least 1 hour or
until dough is firm enough to shape.

2 Preheat oven to 325°F. Line large cookie sheet
with parchment paper. Spread pine nuts on sheet
of waxed paper or in pie plate.

3 Dip hands in water, and then shape dough by
level tablespoons into 1-inch balls. Roll balls in
pine nuts. Place balls, 2 inches apart, on prepared
cookie sheet. Repeat with remaining dough and
pine nuts, wetting hands when necessary to keep
dough from sticking. Bake for 15 to 18 minutes or
until edges are golden and tops begin to brown.
Transfer cookies to wire racks to cool completely.

EACH COOKIE: ABOUT 90 CALORIES, 2G PROTEIN,
10G CARBOHYDRATE, 5G TOTAL FAT (1G SATURATED),
1G FIBER, 0MG CHOLESTEROL, 10MG SODIUM.

TIP

Nuts are highly perishable, so store them
in the refrigerator (or freezer). If you're
working with a stash that's been kept at
room temperature, always taste a nut first to
make sure it hasn't gone rancid.

BEST
Linzer Cookies

We take the classic flavor combo of Austrian linzer torte—toasted nuts and raspberry—to craft melt-in-your-mouth treats of exceptional beauty and flavor.

ACTIVE TIME: 1½ HOURS   **TOTAL TIME:** 2 HOURS 10 MINUTES PLUS CHILLING AND COOLING
MAKES: ABOUT 4 DOZEN COOKIES

1   bag (8 ounces) pecans (about 2 cups)

½   cup cornstarch

1½ cups (3 sticks) butter, softened

1⅓ cups confectioners' sugar

2   teaspoons vanilla extract

¾   teaspoon salt

1   large egg

2¾ cups all-purpose flour

¾   cup seedless red raspberry jam

1 In food processor with knife blade attached, pulse pecans and cornstarch until pecans are finely ground.

2 In large bowl with mixer on low speed, beat butter and 1 cup confectioners' sugar until mixed. Increase speed to high; beat for 2 minutes or until light and fluffy, occasionally scraping bowl with rubber spatula. Reduce speed to medium; beat in vanilla, salt, and egg. Reduce speed to low; gradually beat in flour and pecan mixture just until blended, occasionally scraping bowl with rubber spatula.

3 Divide dough into 4 equal pieces; flatten each into a disk. Wrap each disk in plastic wrap and refrigerate for 4 to 5 hours or until dough is firm enough to roll.

4 Preheat oven to 325°F. Remove 1 disk of dough from refrigerator; if necessary, let stand for 10 to 15 minutes at room temperature for easier rolling. On lightly floured surface, with floured rolling pin, roll dough ⅛-inch thick. With floured 2¼-inch fluted round, plain round, or holiday-shaped cookie cutter, cut dough into as many cookies as possible. With floured 1- to 1¼-inch fluted round, plain round, or holiday-shaped cookie cutter, cut out centers from half of cookies. Wrap and refrigerate trimmings. With lightly floured spatula, carefully place cookies, 1 inch apart, on large ungreased cookie sheet.

5 Bake cookies for 17 to 20 minutes or until edges are lightly browned. With spatula, transfer cookies to wire racks to cool completely. Repeat with remaining dough and trimmings.

6 When cookies are cool, sift remaining ⅓ cup confectioners' sugar over cookies with cutout centers.

7 In small bowl, stir jam with fork until smooth. Spread scant measuring teaspoons of jam on top of whole cookies; place cutout cookies on top.

EACH COOKIE: ABOUT 115 CALORIES, 1G PROTEIN, 11G CARBOHYDRATE, 8G TOTAL FAT (3G SATURATED), 1G FIBER, 17MG CHOLESTEROL, 80MG SODIUM.

Spritz COOKIES

The name spritz comes from the German word *spritzen*—
meaning "to squirt"—because the soft, buttery dough
is pushed through a cookie press to make fancy designs.

ACTIVE TIME: 35 MINUTES   **TOTAL TIME:** 1 HOUR PLUS COOLING   **MAKES:** ABOUT 5½ DOZEN COOKIES

2¼ cups all-purpose flour

½   teaspoon baking powder

½   teaspoon salt

1   cup (2 sticks) butter or margarine, softened

½   cup granulated sugar

1   large egg

1   teaspoon vanilla extract

1   teaspoon almond extract

Candy decors, optional

Ornamental Frosting (page 18), optional

1 Preheat oven to 350°F. Place three cookie sheets in freezer.

2 In medium bowl with wire whisk, combine flour, baking powder, and salt.

3 In large bowl with mixer on medium speed, beat butter and sugar until light and fluffy. Beat in egg, then beat in extracts. Reduce speed to low; gradually beat in flour mixture just until blended, occasionally scraping bowl with rubber spatula.

4 Spoon one-third of dough into cookie press or large decorating bag fitted with large star tip. Onto 1 chilled cookie sheet, press or pipe dough into desired shapes, spacing 2 inches apart. Sprinkle with candy decors, if desired.

5 Bake for 10 to 12 minutes or until lightly browned around edges. Cool cookies on cookie sheet on wire rack for 2 minutes. With spatula, transfer cookies to wire racks to cool completely. Repeat with remaining dough and chilled cookie sheets.

6 When cookies are cool, prepare Ornamental Frosting, if desired; use to decorate cookies. Set cookies aside to allow frosting to dry.

EACH COOKIE: ABOUT 50 CALORIES, 1G PROTEIN, 5G CARBOHYDRATE, 3G TOTAL FAT (2G SATURATED), 0G FIBER, 10MG CHOLESTEROL, 20MG SODIUM.

LEBKUCHEN

We transformed these classic German cut-out cookies
into easy-bake bars and added a lemony icing.

ACTIVE TIME: 15 MINUTES   TOTAL TIME: 45 MINUTES PLUS COOLING AND STANDING   MAKES: 64 BARS

1   box (16 ounces) dark brown sugar
    (2¼ cups packed)

4   large eggs

1½ cups all-purpose flour

1½ teaspoons ground cinnamon

1   teaspoon baking powder

¾   teaspoon ground cloves

1   cup walnuts, coarsely chopped

1   cup dark seedless raisins or ¾ cup diced
    mixed candied fruit

½   cup confectioners' sugar

1   tablespoon fresh lemon juice

1   Preheat oven to 350°F. Line 13" by 9" baking
pan with foil, extending over rim. Spray foil with
nonstick baking spray.

2   In large bowl with mixer at medium speed,
beat brown sugar and eggs until well mixed,
about 1 minute, occasionally scraping bowl with
rubber spatula. Reduce speed to low; gradually
beat in flour, cinnamon, baking powder, and
cloves just until blended, occasionally scraping
bowl. Stir in walnuts and raisins.

3   Spoon mixture into prepared pan and spread
evenly. Bake for 30 minutes. Cool completely in
pan on wire rack.

4   In medium bowl, mix confectioners' sugar and
lemon juice. Drizzle sugar icing over Lebkuchen.
Let stand for 10 minutes or until icing is set.
Using foil, remove bar from pan. Cut lengthwise
into 8 strips, then cut each strip crosswise into
8 bars.

EACH BAR: ABOUT 65 CALORIES, 1G PROTEIN,
12G CARBOHYDRATE, 2G TOTAL FAT (0G SATURATED),
0G FIBER, 13MG CHOLESTEROL, 15MG SODIUM.

ENGLISH Tea Cakes

Tea cakes are dainty-sized sweets traditionally served in England with afternoon tea. To simplify things for the holidays, we made them into bars. For photo, see page 46.

For photo, see page 46.

ACTIVE TIME: 30 MINUTES   **TOTAL TIME:** 1 HOUR 20 MINUTES PLUS COOLING AND CHILLING
MAKES: 64 BARS

TEA CAKES

- ¼ cup confectioners' sugar
- 1 cup plus 2 tablespoons all-purpose flour
- ½ cup (1 stick) cold butter
- 2 large eggs
- 1½ cups packed brown sugar
- 1 cup coarsely chopped pecans or walnuts
- ½ cup sweetened flaked coconut
- 1 teaspoon vanilla extract
- ½ teaspoon salt
- ¼ teaspoon baking powder

LEMON BUTTER FROSTING

- 1 lemon
- 1 cup confectioners' sugar
- 6 tablespoons butter, softened

1 Preheat oven to 350°F. Line 9" by 9" baking pan with foil, extending over rim.

2 Prepare Tea Cakes: In medium bowl with wire whisk, combine confectioners' sugar and 1 cup flour. With pastry blender or 2 knives used scissors-fashion, cut in butter until mixture resembles coarse crumbs. With fingertips, press mixture evenly onto bottom of prepared pan. Bake crust for 23 to 25 minutes or until lightly browned. Remove pan from oven.

3 While crust bakes, in same medium bowl, with fork, mix eggs, brown sugar, nuts, coconut, vanilla, salt, baking powder, and remaining 2 tablespoons flour until well blended.

4 Spread topping evenly over hot crust. Return pan to oven; bake for 25 minutes more, or until topping is just set and edges are golden. Cool completely in pan on wire rack.

5 Prepare Lemon Butter Frosting: From lemon, grate 1 teaspoon peel and squeeze 4 teaspoons juice. In medium bowl with mixer on medium speed, beat lemon peel and juice, confectioners' sugar, and butter until smooth. Spread frosting over top of cake. Refrigerate for 10 to 15 minutes or until frosting is slightly firm for easier cutting.

6 Using foil, remove bar from pan. Cut into 8 strips, then cut each strip crosswise into 8 bars.

EACH COOKIE: ABOUT 75 CALORIES, 1G PROTEIN, 10G CARBOHYDRATE, 4G TOTAL FAT (2G SATURATED), 0G FIBER, 14MG CHOLESTEROL, 50MG SODIUM.

TIP

To make grating citrus easier, choose a pebbly textured (versus smooth), thick-skinned lemon for this recipe.

Salted Toffee RUGELACH

Toffee bits and roasted salted almonds give
these classic cookies from Russia a modern twist.

ACTIVE TIME: 30 MINUTES   TOTAL TIME: 1 HOUR 10 MINUTES PLUS CHILLING AND COOLING
MAKES: 4 DOZEN COOKIES

1   cup (2 sticks) butter, softened

1   package (8 ounces) full-fat cream cheese,
    softened

1   teaspoon vanilla extract

3   tablespoons plus ¼ cup packed brown sugar

2   cups all-purpose flour

½   teaspoon salt

1   cup toffee bits

¾   cup roasted salted almonds, finely chopped

Confectioners' sugar

1   Arrange oven racks in top and bottom thirds
of oven. Preheat oven to 350°F. Line two large
cookie sheets with parchment paper.

2   In large bowl with mixer on medium speed,
beat butter, cream cheese, vanilla, and 3
tablespoons brown sugar until well mixed.
Reduce speed to low; gradually beat in flour and
salt just until blended, occasionally scraping bowl
with rubber spatula. Shape dough into 4 equal-
sized disks. Wrap in plastic wrap and refrigerate
for at least 2 hours or up to 24 hours, until dough
is firm enough to roll.

3   Meanwhile, in medium bowl, combine toffee,
almonds, and remaining ¼ cup brown sugar.

4   On well-floured, large sheet of parchment
paper, with floured rolling pin, roll 1 disk of
dough into 9-inch circle. Sprinkle with one-
quarter of toffee mixture, leaving ½-inch rim.
Gently press filling into dough. With sharp knife
or pastry cutter, cut circle into 12 equal wedges.
Starting at outer edge, roll each wedge into a
crescent. (If dough becomes too soft or sticky to
roll, place parchment and dough on cookie sheet
and refrigerate for 10 minutes, or until firmer but
still pliable.) Place, point sides down, on prepared
cookie sheet, spacing 1 inch apart. Bake for 20
minutes or until golden brown, rotating cookie
sheets between upper and lower racks halfway
through baking.

5   Slide cookies, still on parchment, onto wire
rack to cool completely. Repeat with remaining
disks of dough, toffee mixture, and cooled, newly
lined cookie sheets. Sift confectioners' sugar over
cooled cookies.

EACH COOKIE: ABOUT 120 CALORIES, 1G PROTEIN,
10G CARBOHYDRATE, 8G TOTAL FAT (4G SATURATED),
0G FIBER, 17MG CHOLESTEROL, 105MG SODIUM.

Apple Pie RUGELACH

A double dose of apples and cinnamon sugar in the filling
make these flaky morsels irresistibly delicious.

ACTIVE TIME: 1 HOUR 30 MINUTES   **TOTAL TIME:** 2 HOUR PLUS CHILLING AND COOLING
MAKES: 64 COOKIES

- 1   cup (2 sticks) butter, softened
- 1   package (8 ounces) full-fat cream cheese, softened
- ¼   cup packed brown sugar
- 2   cups all-purpose flour
- ½   teaspoon salt
- 4   ounces finely chopped dried apples
- ½   cup finely choped walnuts
- 1   cup granulated sugar
- 2   teaspoons ground cinnamon
- 12 tablespoons apple jelly

1 Arrange oven racks in top and bottom thirds of oven. Preheat oven to 350°F. Line two large cookie sheets with parchment paper.

2 In large bowl with mixer on medium speed, beat butter, cream cheese, and brown sugar until well mixed. Reduce speed to low; gradually beat in flour and salt just until blended, occasionally scraping bowl with rubber spatula. Shape dough into 4 equal-sized disks. Wrap in plastic wrap and refrigerate for at least 2 hours or up to 24 hours, until dough is firm enough to roll.

3 Meanwhile, in medium bowl, combine dried apples and walnuts. In small bowl, combine granulated sugar and cinnamon.

4 Sprinkle work surface with 2 tablespoons cinnamon sugar. Place 1 disk dough on top of sugar; turn over to coat both sides. Roll dough into 10-inch circle, turning circle over a few times and sprinkling dough with 2 more tablespoons cinnamon sugar to coat both sides. Spread top of circle with 3 tablespoons apple jelly, then sprinkle with ½ cup apple mixture, leaving ½-inch rim. Cut dough into 16 equal wedges. Starting at outer edge, roll each wedge into crescent. (If dough becomes too soft or sticky to roll, place parchment with dough on cookie sheet and refrigerate for 10 minutes or until firmer but still pliable.) Place, point sides down, on prepared cookie sheet, spacing 1 inch apart. Bake for 30 to 33 minutes or until golden brown, rotating cookie sheets between upper and lower racks halfway through baking.

5 Slide cookies, still on parchment, onto wire rack to cool completely. Repeat with remaining disks of dough, cinnamon sugar, 9 tablespoons apple jelly, apple mixture, and cooled, newly lined cookie sheets. Sift confectioners' sugar over cooled cookies.

EACH COOKIE: ABOUT 90 CALORIES, 1G PROTEIN, 11G CARBOHYDRATE, 5G TOTAL FAT (3G SATURATED), 0G FIBER, 12MG CHOLESTEROL, 40MG SODIUM.

Walnut BALLS

A global favorite (also known as Mexican wedding cakes
or Russian tea cakes), these nutty morsels earn
their privileged position on the holiday cookie tray.
Use ground almonds or pecans, if you prefer.

ACTIVE TIME: 45 MINUTES   **TOTAL TIME:** 1 HOUR 30 MINUTES PLUS COOLING   **MAKES:** 6½ DOZEN COOKIES

1   **cup (2 sticks) butter, softened**

6   **tablespoons granulated sugar**

½   **teaspoon vanilla extract**

2   **cups all-purpose flour**

⅛   **teaspoon salt**

1   **bag (8 ounces) walnuts, chopped**

1¼   **cups confectioners' sugar**

1   Preheat oven to 325°F. In large bowl with mixer on medium speed, beat butter, granulated sugar, and vanilla until light and fluffy, occasionally scraping bowl with rubber spatula. Reduce speed to low; gradually beat in flour and salt just until blended, occasionally scraping bowl. Stir in walnuts.

2 Shape dough by rounded measuring teaspoons into 1-inch balls. Place balls, 1 inch apart, on large ungreased cookie sheet. Bake for 13 to 15 minutes or until bottoms are lightly browned.

3 Place confectioners' sugar in pie plate. While cookies are hot, with spatula, transfer 4 or 5 cookies at a time to pie plate with confectioners' sugar. Gently turn cookies with fork to generously coat with sugar. Transfer cookies to wire racks to cool completely. Repeat with remaining dough and confectioners' sugar.

EACH COOKIE: ABOUT 65 CALORIES, 1G PROTEIN, 6G CARBOHYDRATE, 4G TOTAL FAT (2G SATURATED), 0G FIBER, 7MG CHOLESTEROL, 30MG SODIUM.

TIP

After turning off the oven post-baking, wash the cookie sheets by hand and place in the warm oven to quickly dry. This also works for baking pans turned upside down in the oven.

"Candy" Bars
(page 76)

4 Bar Beauties

If the idea of making dozens of holiday cookies using only one pan sounds appealing, this collection of bar cookies is custom-made for you. Chocoholics will love our "Candy" Bars and Coconut Joy Bars. If you've been invited to a cookie swap, big-batch recipes like our Orange-Ginger Bars, Pistachio Thins, or Butter-Almond Thins are perfect for sharing.

For the best bar cookies, be sure to use the correct pan size specified in the recipe. A pan that's too small will cause your bars to be too thick and gummy; too large a pan will produce thin, dried-out bars. We also recommend using metal baking pans, because glass absorbs and retains more heat, which can cause the bars to overbake.

PB & J BARS

These homey bar cookies are sure to bring lots of holiday cheer.

ACTIVE TIME: 15 MINUTES   **TOTAL TIME:** 10 MINUTES PLUS COOLING   **MAKES:** 3½ DOZEN BARS

¾ cup (1½ sticks) butter, softened

½ cup packed brown sugar

½ teaspoon salt

1 large egg

1½ teaspoons vanilla extract

2 cups all-purpose flour

¾ cup strawberry jam

¾ cup peanut butter chips

1 Preheat oven to 375°F. Line 13" by 9" baking pan with foil, extending over rim. Spray foil with nonstick baking spray.

2 In large bowl with mixer on medium-high speed, beat butter, brown sugar, and salt until light and fluffy. Beat in egg and vanilla. Reduce speed to low; gradually beat in flour just until blended, occasionally scraping bowl with rubber spatula. Transfer to prepared pan. With lightly floured hands, spread dough into even layer.

3 Bake for 25 to 30 minutes or until deep golden brown around edges. Cool for about 10 minutes. Spread warm crust with jam; top evenly with peanut butter chips. Cool completely in pan on wire rack.

4 Using foil, remove bar from pan. Cut into 1-inch squares.

EACH BAR: ABOUT 93 CALORIES, 1G PROTEIN, 12G CARBOHYDRATE, 4G TOTAL FAT (3G SATURATED), 0G FIBER, 13MG CHOLESTEROL, 60MG SODIUM.

TIP

To cut bar cookies like a pro, use a ruler as your guide. Mark the sides of the bar with toothpicks, and then cut into cookies with a long sharp or serrated knife.

Clockwise from top left:
PB & J Bars (opposite), Brown
Sugar-Hazelnut Bars (page 72),
Pistachio Thins (page 73), Apricot
Crumb Bars (page 75)

Brown Sugar-Hazelnut BARS

Layers of chocolate-hazelnut spread and toasted chopped nuts mean a double dose of hazelnuts in every luscious bar. For photo, see page 71.

ACTIVE TIME: 15 MINUTES   **TOTAL TIME:** 40 MINUTES PLUS COOLING   **MAKES:** ABOUT 3 DOZEN BARS

¾ cup (1½ sticks) butter, softened

½ cup packed brown sugar

½ teaspoon salt

1 large egg

1½ teaspoons vanilla extract

2 cups all-purpose flour

½ cup chocolate-hazelnut spread

1 cup hazelnuts, toasted, skinned, and chopped

1 Preheat oven to 375°F. Line 13" by 9" baking pan with foil, extending over rim. Spray foil with nonstick baking spray.

2 In large bowl with mixer on medium-high speed, beat butter, brown sugar, and salt until light and fluffy. Beat in egg and vanilla. Reduce speed to low; gradually beat in flour just until blended, occasionally scraping bowl with rubber spatula. Transfer dough to prepared pan. With lightly floured hands, spread into even layer.

3 Bake for 25 to 30 minutes or until deep golden brown around edges. Cool completely in pan on wire rack.

4 Spread cooled crust with chocolate-hazelnut spread. Sprinkle with hazelnuts; press to adhere. Using foil, remove bar from pan. Cut into 1½-inch squares.

EACH BAR: ABOUT 100 CALORIES, 1G PROTEIN, 10G CARBOHYDRATE, 6G TOTAL FAT (3G SATURATED), 1G FIBER, 13MG CHOLESTEROL, 30MG SODIUM.

Hazelnut How-To

Toasting hazelnuts accomplishes two things: it intensifies the natural sweetness of the nuts, and it enables you to easily remove the thin, mildly bitter skins. Follow these steps when making our Brown Sugar-Hazelnut Bars (above), Cherry Linzer Bars (page 81), or Hazelnut-Chocolate Sandwich cookies (page 96).

- **Spread** hazelnuts in single layer on rimmed baking sheet; bake at 350°F for 12 to 15 minutes or until lightly browned and skins are crackly.
- **Wrap** nuts in clean kitchen towel and let stand for 5 minutes.
- **Rub** nuts in towel to remove skins, then cool completely.

Pistachio THINS

These heavenly spiced crisp cookies couldn't be easier to prepare.
For photo, see page 71.

ACTIVE TIME: 15 MINUTES   **TOTAL TIME:** 30 MINUTES PLUS COOLING   **MAKES:** ABOUT 4 DOZEN COOKIES

¾ cup (1½ sticks) butter, softened

½ cup packed brown sugar

½ teaspoon salt

½ teaspoon ground cinnamon

¼ teaspoon ground nutmeg

1 large egg

1½ teaspoons vanilla extract

2 cups all-purpose flour

½ cup pistachios, very finely chopped

1 Preheat oven to 375°F. Line 18" by 12" rimmed baking sheet with foil, extending over rim. Spray foil with nonstick baking spray.

2 In large bowl with mixer on medium-high speed, beat butter, brown sugar, salt, cinnamon, and nutmeg until light and fluffy. Beat in egg and vanilla. Reduce speed to low; gradually beat in flour just until blended, scraping bowl occasionally with rubber spatula. Transfer to prepared pan. With lightly floured hands, press dough into very thin, even layer. Sprinkle with pistachios and press nuts into the dough.

3 With pizza cutter or very sharp knife, cut dough lengthwise into 3-inch-wide rectangles, then crosswise to form 3-inch squares. Cut squares diagonally into triangles.

4 Bake for 15 to 17 minutes or until golden. Cool completely in pan on wire rack. Gently break triangles to separate.

EACH COOKIE: ABOUT 62 CALORIES, 1G PROTEIN, 7G CARBOHYDRATE, 4G TOTAL FAT (2G SATURATED), 0G FIBER, 12MG CHOLESTEROL, 46MG SODIUM.

TIP

Bar cookies (cut or uncut) can be stored in their baking pan covered with a layer of plastic wrap and foil.

Apricot Crumb BARS

This holiday keeper features a cinnamon-scented shortbread crust topped with apricot jam and buttery crumbs. You can also use seedless raspberry jam.

ACTIVE TIME: 15 MINUTES   **TOTAL TIME:** 35 MINUTES PLUS COOLING   **MAKES:** ABOUT 2 DOZEN BARS

TOPPING

- ½ cup all-purpose flour
- ¼ cup packed brown sugar
- 3 tablespoons butter, softened
- ¼ teaspoon ground cinnamon

BARS

- ¾ cup (1½ sticks) butter, softened
- ½ cup packed brown sugar
- ½ teaspoon salt
- 1 large egg
- 1½ teaspoons vanilla extract
- 2 cups all-purpose flour
- ¾ cup apricot jam

1 Preheat oven to 375°F. Line 13" by 9" baking pan with foil, extending over rim. Spray foil with nonstick baking spray.

2 **Prepare Topping:** In medium bowl, combine flour, brown sugar, butter, and cinnamon; pinch with fingers until clumps form.

3 **Prepare Bars:** In large bowl with mixer on medium-high speed, beat butter, brown sugar, and salt until light and fluffy. Beat in egg and vanilla. Reduce speed to low; gradually beat in flour just until blended, scraping bowl occasionally with rubber spatula. Transfer to prepared pan. With lightly floured hands, spread dough into even layer.

4 Bake for 15 minutes or until golden. Spread hot crust with ¾ cup apricot jam; sprinkle with topping. Bake for 20 minutes more or until top is golden brown. Cool completely in pan on wire rack.

5 Using foil, remove bar from pan. Cut into 2-inch squares.

EACH BAR: ABOUT 165 CALORIES, 2G PROTEIN, 23G CARBOHYDRATE, 8G TOTAL FAT (5G SATURATED), 0.5G FIBER, 27MG CHOLESTEROL, 107MG SODIUM.

"Candy" BARS

Kids will love the caramel topping with toffee bits, pretzels, coconut, and melted chocolate. For photo, see page 68.

ACTIVE TIME: 15 MINUTES · **TOTAL TIME:** 45 MINUTES PLUS COOLING AND CHILLING
MAKES: ABOUT 2 DOZEN BARS

¾ cup (1½ sticks) butter, softened

½ cup packed brown sugar

½ teaspoon salt

1 large egg

1½ teaspoons vanilla extract

2 cups all-purpose flour

¾ cup caramel sauce

¼ cup toffee bits

¼ cup broken pretzels

½ cup sweetened flaked coconut, toasted

4 ounces bittersweet chocolate, melted

1 Preheat oven to 375°F. Line 13" by 9" baking pan with foil, extending over rim. Spray foil with nonstick baking spray.

2 In large bowl with mixer on medium-high speed, beat butter, brown sugar, and salt until light and fluffy. Beat in egg and vanilla. Reduce speed to low; gradually beat in flour just until blended, scraping bowl occasionally with rubber spatula.

3 Transfer to prepared pan. With lightly floured hands, spread dough into even layer. Bake for 25 to 30 minutes or until deep golden brown around edges. Cool completely in pan on wire rack.

4 Spread cooled crust with caramel sauce. Top evenly with toffee bits, pretzels, and coconut; press to adhere. Drizzle with melted chocolate. Refrigerate until chocolate sets, about 1½ hours. Using foil, remove bar from pan. Cut into 2-inch squares.

EACH BAR: ABOUT 183 CALORIES, 2G PROTEIN, 24G CARBOHYDRATE, 10G TOTAL FAT (6G SATURATED), 1G FIBER, 24MG CHOLESTEROL, 146MG SODIUM.

SESAME-ALMOND
Squares

Talk about easy! These ultrarich squares have only five ingredients, including store-bought graham crackers.

ACTIVE TIME: 10 MINUTES **TOTAL TIME:** 30 MINUTES PLUS COOLING **MAKES:** ABOUT 2 DOZEN BARS

12 graham crackers (5" by 2½" each)

¾ cup butter (1½ sticks), cut up

½ cup granulated sugar

1 cup sliced almonds

2 tablespoons sesame seeds

1 Preheat oven to 350°F. Place graham crackers side by side in ungreased 15½" by 10½" rimmed baking sheet. (Make sure to use pan size called for. Crackers should cover entire pan with no spaces in between.)

2 In 1-quart saucepan, combine butter and sugar; heat to boiling over medium-low heat, stirring occasionally. Boil for 2 minutes or until mixture thickens slightly. Spread mixture evenly over graham crackers; sprinkle with almonds and sesame seeds.

3 Bake for 18 to 19 minutes or until crackers brown slightly and butter bubbles and turns golden. Watch carefully during last 2 to 3 minutes of baking to make sure graham crackers do not overbrown.

4 While bars are still in pan, immediately cut graham cracker crosswise in half. With metal spatula, transfer cookies to wire rack to cool.

EACH BAR: ABOUT 130 CALORIES, 2G PROTEIN, 11G CARBOHYDRATE, 10G TOTAL FAT (4G SATURATED), 1G FIBER, 16MG CHOLESTEROL, 105MG SODIUM.

Butter-Almond THINS

Nut lovers will adore these crisp morsels with cardamom
and a toasted almond topping. They're the perfect choice
for gift giving. For photo, see page 11.

ACTIVE TIME: 30 MINUTES   **TOTAL TIME:** 50 MINUTES PLUS COOLING   **MAKES:** ABOUT 7 DOZEN COOKIES

3/4 cup (1½ sticks) butter, softened

⅓ cup granulated sugar

½ teaspoon ground cardamom

¼ teaspoon salt

1 large egg, separated

1 teaspoon almond extract

1 teaspoon vanilla extract

2 cups all-purpose flour

2 cups sliced blanched almonds

4 tablespoons confectioners' sugar

1 Preheat oven to 375°F. Line 18" by 12" rimmed baking sheet with foil, extending over rim. Spray foil with nonstick baking spray.

2 In large bowl with mixer on medium speed, beat butter, granulated sugar, cardamom, and salt until light and fluffy. Beat in egg yolk and extracts until well incorporated. Reduce speed to low; beat in flour just until clumps form.

3 Scatter clumps evenly on prepared pan. With palm and fingertips, press dough into thin, even layer without any gaps.

4 In medium bowl, whisk egg white until frothy; fold in almonds and 2 tablespoons confectioners' sugar. Spread in even layer over dough, pressing into dough gently. With pizza cutter or sharp knife, cut dough crosswise into 2-inch strips; cut each strip crosswise to form 2-inch squares. Cut squares diagonally into triangles. Sift remaining 2 tablespoons confectioners' sugar over tops.

5 Bake for 15 to 18 minutes or until golden brown. Cool completely in pan on wire rack. Carefully break cookies into triangles.

EACH COOKIE: ABOUT 45 CALORIES, 1G PROTEIN, 4G CARBOHYDRATE, 3G TOTAL FAT (1G SATURATED), 0G FIBER, 7MG CHOLESTEROL, 25MG SODIUM.

Coconut Joy BARS

While these cookies get their inspiration from the famous chocolate candies, they're even moister (and less sweet). For photo, see page 11.

ACTIVE TIME: 20 MINUTES   **TOTAL TIME:** 1 HOUR 15 MINUTES PLUS COOLING AND CHILLING
MAKES: ABOUT 4 DOZEN BARS

1   bag (14 ounces) sweetened flaked coconut

1½ cups all-purpose flour

⅓ cup confectioners' sugar

¼ teaspoon salt

1   cup butter (2 sticks), softened

¾ cup granulated sugar

⅓ cup cornstarch

1   can (14 ounces) coconut milk, shaken

8   ounces bittersweet chocolate, chopped

1   Preheat oven to 350°F. In 13" by 9" baking pan, spread 1 cup coconut. Bake for 6 to 8 minutes or until golden, stirring once. Transfer to plate and cool completely.

2   Wipe out baking pan and cool completely. Line pan with foil, extending over rim; lightly grease foil.

3   In food processor with knife blade attached, finely grind toasted coconut. Add flour, confectioners' sugar, and ⅛ teaspoon salt; pulse to blend. Add butter. Pulse until blended.

4   With spatula, spread dough into even layer in prepared pan. Bake for 30 minutes or until golden brown. Cool completely in pan on wire rack.

5   In 2-quart saucepan, whisk granulated sugar, cornstarch, and remaining ⅛ teaspoon salt. Whisk in coconut milk until smooth. Heat to simmering over medium-high heat, whisking frequently. Simmer for 2 minutes or until very thick, whisking. Fold in remaining untoasted coconut. Cool slightly. Spread in even layer over cooled crust.

6   Place chocolate in medium microwave-safe bowl. Microwave on high for 2 minutes (in 30-second intervals) until almost completely melted, stirring between intervals. Stir mixture until smooth. Pour and spread melted chocolate over coconut filling. Refrigerate until chocolate sets. Using foil, remove bar from pan. Cut into 1" by 2" rectangles.

EACH BAR: ABOUT 145 CALORIES, 2G PROTEIN, 14G CARBOHYDRATE, 10G TOTAL FAT (8G SATURATED), 1G FIBER, 10MG CHOLESTEROL, 70MG SODIUM.

TIP

Store these bars in an airtight container in the fridge for up to 3 days.

Cherry Linzer BARS

These festive cookies will remind you of the finest hazelnut Linzer torte, only with a tart cherry filling.

ACTIVE TIME: 45 MINUTES **TOTAL TIME:** 1 HOUR 20 MINUTES PLUS COOLING **MAKES:** 3 DOZEN BARS

½   cup dried cherries

1¾ cups all-purpose flour

1   teaspoon ground cinnamon

½   teaspoon baking powder

¼   teaspoon salt

1   cup hazelnuts, toasted and skinned

½   cup granulated sugar

½   cup packed light brown sugar

¾   cup (1½ sticks) butter, softened

½   teaspoon freshly grated lemon peel

1   large egg

1   jar (12 ounces) cherry jam

Confectioners' sugar

1 Preheat oven to 350°F. In small microwave-safe bowl, combine cherries and *2 tablespoons water*; microwave on high for 1 minute. Set aside.

2 Meanwhile, line 13" by 9" baking pan with foil, extending over rim. In medium bowl with wire whisk, combine flour, cinnamon, baking powder, and salt.

3 In food processor with knife blade attached, pulse nuts and sugars until nuts are finely ground. Add butter and lemon peel; pulse until creamy. Blend in egg. Add flour mixture; pulse just until mixture comes together.

4 Reserve 1¼ cups dough; refrigerate. With floured fingers, press remaining dough into bottom of prepared pan. Stir jam into cherries; spread over crust, up to ¼ inch from edges. With hands, roll chilled dough into ¼-inch-thick ropes; arrange diagonally, 1½ inches apart, over jam. Arrange remaining ropes around edge of pan. Bake for 35 minutes or until dough is golden. Cool completely in pan on wire rack.

5 Using foil, remove bar from pan. Cut into 36 bars, and sift confectioners' sugar over top.

EACH BAR: ABOUT 135 CALORIES, 2G PROTEIN, 19G CARBOHYDRATE, 6G TOTAL FAT (3G SATURATED), 1G FIBER, 15MG CHOLESTEROL, 25MG SODIUM.

White Chocolate-Macadamia BARS

These indulgently delicious bars feature a layer of caramel topped with salted macadamia nuts and chunks of white chocolate.

ACTIVE TIME: 25 MINUTES **TOTAL TIME:** 55 MINUTES PLUS COOLING AND CHILLING **MAKES:** 4 DOZEN BARS

CRUST

2¼ cups all-purpose flour

⅓ cup granulated sugar

¾ cup (1½ sticks) cold butter, cut into ½-inch cubes

FILLING

1½ cups packed dark brown sugar

4 tablespoons butter

3 tablespoons light corn syrup

¼ teaspoon salt

1 can (14 ounces) sweetened condensed milk

2 teaspoons vanilla extract

1½ cups salted macadamia nuts, chopped

1 cup white chocolate chunks

1 Prepare Crust: Preheat oven to 350°F. Line 13" by 9" baking pan with foil, extending over rim. Spray foil with nonstick baking spray.

2 In food processor with knife blade attached, pulse flour and sugar until blended. Add butter and pulse until dough begins to form a ball. Press dough into bottom of prepared pan in even layer. Freeze for 10 minutes.

3 Bake crust for 20 to 25 minutes or until golden brown with darker brown edges. Cool completely in pan on wire rack.

4 Prepare Filling: In 3-quart saucepan, combine brown sugar, butter, corn syrup, *2 tablespoons water*, and salt. Heat to boiling over medium-high heat, stirring occasionally with heatproof rubber spatula. Stir in condensed milk; return to boiling. Reduce heat to medium-low. Simmer for 10 minutes or until caramel mixture thickens slightly, stirring frequently (especially around edges of saucepan) to prevent scorching. Remove from heat; stir in vanilla. Pour caramel over cooled crust, spreading evenly.

5 While caramel is hot, sprinkle with nuts and chocolate. With spatula, gently push nuts into caramel. Cool completely on wire rack. Refrigerate for 30 minutes before cutting. Using foil, remove bar from pan. Cut lengthwise into 6 strips, then crosswise into 8 pieces.

EACH BAR: ABOUT 165 CALORIES, 2G PROTEIN, 21G CARBOHYDRATE, 9G TOTAL FAT (4G SATURATED), 0G FIBER, 14MG CHOLESTEROL, 75MG SODIUM.

TIP

Here's an easy way to even out the dough for the crust: Cover the surface with a large sheet of parchment paper, and then press the dough down with another 13" by 9" baking pan.

Orange-Ginger BARS

Proceed with recipe as directed in steps 1 through 4. Substitute ½ **cup chopped candied orange peel** and ½ **cup chopped crystallized ginger** for macadamia nuts and **1 cup semisweet chocolate chunks** for white chocolate chunks in step 5.

....

EACH BAR: ABOUT 155 CALORIES, 2G PROTEIN, 25G CARBOHYDRATE, 6G TOTAL FAT (4G SATURATED), 1G FIBER, 13MG CHOLESTEROL, 65MG SODIUM.

Razzy-Jammy Thumbprints
(page 86)

5 Filled with Joy

This festive array of cookies has something very special in common: a tasty treat inside. Choices include Razzy-Jammy, Chocolate-Peanut Butter, and Salted Caramel Thumbprints. Or, try your hand at scrumptious sandwich cookies filled with dulce de leche or chocolate-hazelnut spread. And if you really want to impress your guests for the holidays, our Fig Crescents and Apple-Walnut Tartlets are elegant enough to serve solo for dessert.

Razzy-Jammy
THUMBPRINTS

We filled these honey-kissed morsels with raspberry jam,
or you could try orange marmalade instead. For photo, see page 84.

ACTIVE TIME: 25 MINUTES   **TOTAL TIME:** 40 MINUTES PLUS COOLING   **MAKES:** ABOUT 3 DOZEN COOKIES

2¼ cups all-purpose flour

1   teaspoon baking powder

½   teaspoon baking soda

¾   cup (1½ sticks) butter, softened

¾   cup granulated sugar

½   teaspoon salt

1   large egg yolk

2   tablespoons honey

1   teaspoon almond extract

½   teaspoon vanilla extract

½   cup seedless raspberry jam

¼   cup confectioners' sugar, optional

1 Preheat oven to 375°F. Line large cookie sheet with parchment paper.

2 In medium bowl with wire whisk, combine flour, baking powder, and baking soda.

3 In large bowl with mixer on medium-high speed, beat butter, granulated sugar, and salt until light and fluffy. Beat in egg yolk, then honey and extracts until smooth, occasionally scraping bowl with rubber spatula. Reduce speed to low; gradually beat in flour mixture just until blended, occasionally scraping bowl.

4 Using 1-tablespoon cookie scoop or measuring spoon, scoop dough and roll into balls. Place balls, 2 inches apart, on prepared cookie sheet.

With floured finger or rounded end of small wooden spoon, make indentation in center of each ball. Fill indentations with ½ teaspoon jam. Bake for 12 minutes or until golden brown around edges.

5 Cool cookies on cookie sheet for 5 minutes. Slide cookies, still on parchment, onto wire rack to cool completely. Repeat with remaining dough and cooled, newly lined cookie sheet.

6 When cookies have cooled, sift confectioners' sugar over tops, if desired.

EACH COOKIE: ABOUT 95 CALORIES, 1G PROTEIN, 14G CARBOHYDRATE, 4G TOTAL FAT (3G SATURATED), 0G FIBER, 15MG CHOLESTEROL, 95MG SODIUM.

Salted Caramel
THUMBPRINTS

Proceed with recipe as directed in steps 1 through 4, but bake cookies unfilled. Fill cooled cookies with **½ cup dulce de leche** and sprinkle with **flaky sea salt,** if desired.

EACH COOKIE: ABOUT 98 CALORIES, 1G PROTEIN, 14G CARBOHYDRATE, 4G TOTAL FAT (3G SATURATED), 0G FIBER, 17MG CHOLESTEROL, 96MG SODIUM.

Apple-Walnut TARTLETS

Cream cheese in the dough
makes these tartlet crusts extra-flaky.

ACTIVE TIME: 30 MINUTES   **TOTAL TIME:** 1 HOUR 30 MINUTES PLUS COOLING
MAKES: ABOUT 3 DOZEN TARTLETS

DOUGH

- 1   cup (2 sticks) butter, softened
- 1   package (8 ounces) full-fat cream cheese, softened
- 1   teaspoon vanilla extract
- 3   tablespoons packed brown sugar
- 2   cups all-purpose flour
- ½   teaspoon salt

FILLING

- ¾   cup walnuts, finely chopped
- ⅔   cup dried apples, chopped
- ½   cup packed brown sugar
- 1   large egg, beaten
- 1   tablespoon butter, melted
- ¼   teaspoon ground cinnamon

1   Arrange oven racks in top and bottom thirds of oven. Preheat oven to 350°F. Spray two mini muffin pans with nonstick baking spray.

2 Prepare Dough: In large bowl with mixer on medium speed, beat butter, cream cheese, vanilla, and brown sugar until well mixed. Reduce speed to low; beat in flour and salt just until combined. Shape dough into 3 equal-sized disks. Wrap in plastic wrap and refrigerate for at least 2 hours or up to 24 hours, until dough is firm.

3 Prepare Filling: In medium bowl, stir together walnuts, dried apples, brown sugar, egg, melted butter, and cinnamon.

4   Divide each disk of dough into 12 equal-size balls about 1 inch in diameter. Place 1 ball in each cup of prepared pans. Press dough onto bottom and up sides of cup; add 2 teaspoons filling. Repeat with remaining dough and filling.

5   Bake for 18 to 22 minutes or until edges are golden brown, rotating muffin pans between upper and lower racks halfway through baking. Cool in pans on wire racks for 5 minutes. Using small angled spatula or butter knife, loosen edges of tartlets from cups and cool completely on wire racks. Repeat with remaining dough and clean muffin pans.

EACH TARTLET: ABOUT 135 CALORIES, 2G PROTEIN, 11G CARBOHYDRATE, 9G TOTAL FAT (5G SATURATED), 1G FIBER, 27MG CHOLESTEROL, 115MG SODIUM.

Chocolate-Peanut Butter
THUMBPRINTS

Chopped roasted peanuts in the dough and a milk chocolate filling are sure to make these thumbprints a crowd-pleaser.

ACTIVE TIME: 30 MINUTES   **TOTAL TIME:** 1 HOUR PLUS COOLING AND CHILLING
MAKES: ABOUT 6 DOZEN COOKIES

2¾ cups all-purpose flour

½ teaspoon baking soda

¼ teaspoon salt

1   cup (2 sticks) butter or margarine, softened

1   cup granulated sugar

1   large egg

1   teaspoon vanilla extract

⅔ cup creamy peanut butter (sweetened, no-stir variety)

½ cup unsalted roasted peanuts, chopped

8   ounces milk chocolate, melted

1 Arrange oven racks in top and bottom thirds of oven. Preheat oven to 350°F. Line two large cookie sheets with parchment paper.

2 In medium bowl with wire whisk, combine flour, baking soda, and salt. In large bowl with mixer on medium speed, beat butter and sugar until light and fluffy. Add egg, vanilla, and peanut butter; beat until well mixed. Reduce speed to medium-low; gradually beat in flour mixture just until blended, occasionally scraping bowl with rubber spatula.

3 Form dough into 1-inch balls; roll in chopped peanuts. Place balls, 2 inches apart, on prepared cookie sheets. With floured handle end of wooden spoon, make indentation in center of each ball. Bake for 15 minutes or until golden around edges, rotating cookie sheets between upper and lower racks halfway through baking. Cool completely on cookie sheets on wire racks. Repeat with remaining dough and cooled, newly lined cookie sheets.

4 When cookies have cooled, fill indentations with melted chocolate, using a teaspoon. Refrigerate until chocolate sets.

EACH COOKIE: ABOUT 90 CALORIES, 2G PROTEIN, 9G CARBOHYDRATE, 5G TOTAL FAT (3G SATURATED), 1G FIBER, 9MG CHOLESTEROL, 55MG SODIUM.

TIP

If the indentations have puffed in step 3, press down again with the handle end of a wooden spoon while the cookies are still warm.

Tiny Jewel TARTLETS

These jam-filled buttons allow the kids to use their little fingers
to make perfect thumbprints.

ACTIVE TIME: 50 MINUTES **TOTAL TIME:** 1 HOUR 15 MINUTES PLUS CHILLING AND COOLING

MAKES: 12 DOZEN COOKIES

- 1 large egg yolk
- ½ teaspoon vanilla extract
- 1½ cups all-purpose flour
- ½ cup granulated sugar
- ¼ teaspoon salt
- ½ teaspoon freshly grated lemon peel
- ¾ cup (1½ sticks) cold butter, cut up
- ½ cup jam, such as raspberry, strawberry, and/or apricot

1 In small bowl, beat egg yolk and vanilla. In food processor with knife blade attached, pulse flour, sugar, and salt to blend. Add lemon peel and butter and pulse until coarse crumbs form. With processor running, add yolk mixture. Pulse until large, moist clumps form. Press dough together and pat into flat ¾-inch-thick square. Wrap tightly with plastic wrap and refrigerate for at least 2 hours and up to 3 days.

2 Unwrap dough and cut crosswise into ½-inch-wide strips, then cut lengthwise to form ½-inch cubes. Let stand for 15 minutes to soften.

3 Preheat oven to 350°F. Line two cookie sheets with parchment paper.

4 Meanwhile, roll 1 cube into a ball; place on prepared sheet. With finger or end of wooden spoon, make an indentation in center. If dough cracks, roll again. Repeat with remaining cubes, spacing balls 1 inch apart. Refrigerate for 15 minutes or until firm.

5 If jam has seeds or chunks, strain through fine-mesh sieve. Place in small resealable plastic bag; snip tiny hole in one corner.

6 Working with 1 cookie sheet at a time, squeeze jam into indentations in dough. Bake for 12 to 15 minutes or until golden brown. Transfer cookies to wire racks to cool completely. Meanwhile, repeat with remaining sheet.

EACH COOKIE: ABOUT 20 CALORIES, 0G PROTEIN, 2G CARBOHYDRATE, 1G TOTAL FAT (1G SATURATED), 0G FIBER, 4MG CHOLESTEROL, 5MG SODIUM.

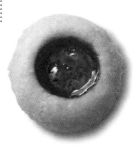

Chocolate-Walnut
THUMBPRINTS

We combined cocoa and melted chocolate in the dough
so these thumbprints are extra fudgy. For photo, see page 11.

ACTIVE TIME: 45 MINUTES   **TOTAL TIME:** 1 HOUR PLUS COOLING   **MAKES:** ABOUT 5 DOZEN COOKIES

1   cup (2 sticks) butter, softened

3/4   cup granulated sugar

1/3   cup unsweetened cocoa

1/4   teaspoon salt

1   large egg, separated

1   teaspoon vanilla extract

2   ounces unsweetened chocolate, melted

2   cups all-purpose flour

1½   cups walnuts, finely chopped

½   cup cherry preserves

1 Preheat oven to 350°F.

2 In large bowl with mixer on low speed, beat butter, sugar, cocoa, and salt until light and fluffy. Beat in egg yolk and vanilla until well blended, occasionally scraping bowl with rubber spatula. Beat in melted chocolate. Add flour and beat just until combined.

3 In small bowl, with fork, beat egg white lightly to break up. Spread walnuts on plate. Roll dough by rounded measuring teaspoons into 1-inch balls. Coat balls lightly in egg white, letting excess drip off. Roll in walnuts to coat. Place cookies, 1½ inches apart, on two large ungreased cookie sheets. With thumb, make indentation in center of each ball.

4 Bake cookies for 8 minutes, switching sheets on racks halfway through baking. Fill each with ¼ teaspoon preserves. Bake for 8 to 10 minutes more, or until jam is bubbly. Let cool on cookie sheets for 2 minutes. With spatula, transfer cookies to wire racks to cool completely.

EACH COOKIE: ABOUT 80 CALORIES, 1G PROTEIN, 8G CARBOHYDRATE, 5G TOTAL FAT (3G SATURATED), 1G FIBER, 11MG CHOLESTEROL, 40MG SODIUM.

Pinwheels

You'll be surprised at how easy it is to shape these festive cookies.
For more variety in both flavor and color, try using
several different kinds of jam.

ACTIVE TIME: 35 MINUTES   **TOTAL TIME:** 45 MINUTES PLUS CHILLING   **MAKES:** 24 COOKIES

1⅓ cups all-purpose flour

¼ teaspoon baking powder

⅛ teaspoon salt

6 tablespoons butter or margarine, softened

½ cup sugar

1 large egg

1 teaspoon vanilla extract

¼ cup damson plum, seedless raspberry, or other jam

1 On sheet of waxed paper, stir together flour, baking powder, and salt.

2 In large bowl, with mixer on medium speed, beat butter and sugar until light and fluffy. Beat in egg and vanilla until well combined. Reduce

speed to low and beat in flour mixture until combined. Divide dough in half, wrap each half in waxed paper, and refrigerate for at least 1 hour, or up to overnight. (If using margarine, freeze overnight.)

3 Preheat oven to 375°F. Remove 1 piece dough from refrigerator. On floured surface, with floured rolling pin, roll dough into 10" by 7½" rectangle. With jagged-edged pastry wheel or sharp knife, cut rectangle lengthwise into 4 strips, then cut each strip into 3 squares. Arrange squares 1 inch apart on two ungreased large cookie sheets. On each square, use small sharp knife to make 1½-inch cut from each corner toward center. Spoon ½ teaspoon jam in center of each square. Fold every other tip into center to form pinwheel.

4 Bake for 9 minutes, or until lightly browned around edges and set, rotating cookie sheets between upper and lower oven racks halfway through. With wide metal spatula, transfer cookies to wire racks to cool completely. Repeat with remaining dough and jam.

5 Store cookies in airtight container, with waxed paper between layers, for up to 3 days, or freeze for up to 3 months.

EACH COOKIE: ABOUT 80 CALORIES, 1G PROTEIN, 12G CARBOHYDRATE, 3G TOTAL FAT (2G SATURATED), 0G FIBER, 17MG CHOLESTEROL, 50MG SODIUM.

FIG **Crescents**

Want to bake a holiday cookie that's sure to impress? Look no further—these fruit-and-nut-filled mini pastries are truly exceptional.

ACTIVE TIME: 1 HOUR 15 MINUTES   **TOTAL TIME:** 1 HOUR 30 MINUTES PLUS CHILLING AND COOLING
MAKES: ABOUT 5½ DOZEN COOKIES

COOKIE DOUGH

2¾ cups all-purpose flour

½ teaspoon salt

¼ teaspoon baking soda

2 large eggs

½ cup (1 stick) butter or margarine, softened

1 cup granulated sugar

2 tablespoons heavy or whipping cream

1 teaspoon vanilla extract

FIG FILLING

1 large orange

5 ounces (¾ cup) dried Mission figs, stems removed

½ cup walnuts

¼ cup raisins

¼ cup honey

1½ teaspoons ground cinnamon

1 large egg

¼ cup white sugar crystals

1 Prepare Cookie Dough: In medium bowl with wire whisk, combine flour, salt, and baking soda. In large bowl, with mixer on medium speed, beat eggs, butter, and granulated sugar for 2 minutes or until creamy, occasionally scraping bowl with rubber spatula. Beat in cream and vanilla until mixed. Reduce speed to low; gradually beat in flour mixture just until blended, occasionally scraping bowl. Divide dough into 4 equal pieces; flatten each into a disk. Wrap each disk in plastic wrap; refrigerate for at least 2 hours or up to 3 days, until dough is firm enough to roll.

2 Prepare Fig Filling: Meanwhile, from orange, finely grate ½ teaspoon peel and squeeze 3 tablespoons juice. In food processor with knife blade attached, pulse orange peel and juice, figs, walnuts, raisins, honey, and cinnamon until coarsely ground.

3 Preheat oven to 350°F. Grease two large cookie sheets. In cup, with fork, lightly beat egg.

4 On lightly floured surface, with floured rolling pin, roll 1 disk of dough ⅛-inch thick. With floured 2½-inch fluted round biscuit or cookie cutter, cut out as many rounds as possible; wrap and refrigerate trimmings. With spatula, carefully transfer rounds, 1 inch apart, to prepared cookie sheets. Spoon 1 level teaspoon of filling onto one side of each round. Fold dough in half over filling. Gently press edges to seal. Lightly brush crescents with egg; sprinkle with white sugar.

5 Bake for 15 to 16 minutes or until tops are golden brown. With spatula, transfer cookies to wire racks to cool completely. Repeat with remaining dough, trimmings, filling, egg, and white sugar.

EACH COOKIE: ABOUT 70 CALORIES, 1G PROTEIN, 11G CARBOHYDRATE, 2G TOTAL FAT (1G SATURATED), 1G FIBER, 13MG CHOLESTEROL, 25MG SODIUM.

Dulce de Leche
SANDWICHES

Cornstarch in the cookie dough makes these treats extra tender.

ACTIVE TIME: 40 MINUTES   **TOTAL TIME:** 1 HOUR PLUS COOLING   **MAKES:** ABOUT 3 DOZEN COOKIES

1   cup all-purpose flour

1²/₃ cups cornstarch

1   teaspoon baking powder

³/₄   teaspoon ground cinnamon

¹/₄   teaspoon salt

10   tablespoons butter, softened

¹/₂   cup granulated sugar

¹/₂   teaspoon vanilla extract

4   large egg yolks

1   jar (16 ounces) dulce de leche

1 Preheat oven to 350°F. Line large cookie sheet with parchment paper.

2 In large bowl, sift flour, cornstarch, baking powder, cinnamon, and salt. In another large bowl with mixer on medium-high speed, beat butter and sugar until light and fluffy. Beat in vanilla, then egg yolks, one at a time. Reduce speed to low; gradually beat in flour mixture just until blended, occasionally scraping bowl with rubber spatula.

3 On lightly floured surface, with lightly floured rolling pin, roll half of dough to ¼-inch thickness. With 1½-inch plain round cutter, cut out rounds. With small knife or mini offset spatula, transfer rounds, 1 inch apart, to prepared cookie sheet. Reroll scraps once. Bake for 12 to 15 minutes or until golden brown on bottoms.

4 Cool cookies on cookie sheet for 5 minutes. Slide cookies, still on parchment, onto wire rack to cool completely. Repeat with remaining dough and cooled, newly lined cookie sheet.

5 To assemble, place dulce de leche in piping bag fitted with star tip. Pipe onto half of cooled cookies. Top with remaining cookies.

EACH COOKIE: ABOUT 120 CALORIES, 2G PROTEIN, 18G CARBOHYDRATE, 5G TOTAL FAT (3G SATURATED), 0G FIBER, 33MG CHOLESTEROL, 75MG SODIUM.

TIP

Dulce de leche is made of sugar and milk (or just sweetened condensed milk) that's been cooked for hours until the mixture becomes very thick and deeply golden in color. Look for it in Latin markets.

Hazelnut-Chocolate
SANDWICH COOKIES

These elegant cookies served with coffee
would make the perfect finale to any holiday feast.

ACTIVE TIME: 50 MINUTES   TOTAL TIME: 1 HOUR 30 MINUTES PLUS COOLING   MAKES: 6 DOZEN COOKIES

2¾ cups all-purpose flour

¼ teaspoon baking soda

¼ teaspoon salt

1 cup (2 sticks) butter, softened

¾ cup granulated sugar

1 large egg

1 teaspoon vanilla extract

⅓ cup hazelnuts, toasted, skinned, and chopped

¾ cup hazelnut-chocolate spread

1 Preheat oven to 350°F. In medium bowl with wire whisk, combine flour, baking soda, and salt.

2 In large bowl with mixer on medium speed, beat butter and sugar for 1 minute or until light and fluffy, occasionally scraping bowl with rubber spatula. Add egg and vanilla; beat until well mixed. Reduce speed to low; gradually beat in flour mixture just until blended, occasionally scraping bowl.

3 With hands, shape dough by level measuring ½ teaspoons into balls. Place balls, 2 inches apart, on large ungreased cookie sheet. Dip bottom of flat-bottomed glass in sugar as needed; use to press each ball into 1-inch round. Sprinkle half of rounds with hazelnuts. Bake for 9 to 10 minutes or until edges are golden brown. With spatula, transfer cookies to wire racks to cool completely. Repeat with remaining dough and hazelnuts.

4 To assemble, spread flat sides of plain cookies with ½ teaspoon hazelnut-chocolate spread. Top each with a nut-covered cookie, top side up, pressing lightly.

EACH COOKIE: ABOUT 65 CALORIES 1G PROTEIN, 7G CARBOHYDRATE, 4G TOTAL FAT (2G SATURATED), 0G FIBER, 10MG CHOLESTEROL, 45MG SODIUM.

TIP

Look for hazelnut-chocolate spread in the same aisle as peanut butter at the supermarket.

COOKIE S'mores

The best parts of s'mores, namely the
melted chocolate and marshmallow, are sandwiched
between tender cinnamon cookies.

ACTIVE TIME: 35 MINUTES   TOTAL TIME: 1 HOUR 10 MINUTES PLUS COOLING AND CHILLING
MAKES: ABOUT 3 DOZEN COOKIES

1   cup (2 sticks) butter, softened

1   package (8 ounces) full-fat cream cheese,
    softened

1   cup granulated sugar

1½ teaspoons ground cinnamon

Salt

1   large egg yolk

1½ teaspoons vanilla extract

2½ cups all-purpose flour

3   ounces semisweet chocolate, melted

½   cup marshmallow crème

1 Preheat oven to 375°F.

2 In large bowl with mixer on medium-
high speed, beat butter, cream cheese, sugar,
cinnamon, and ½ teaspoon salt until light and
fluffy. Beat in egg yolk and vanilla, occasionally
scraping bowl with rubber spatula. Reduce speed
to low; gradually beat in flour just until blended,
occasionally scraping bowl.

3 Using 1-tablespoon cookie scoop or measuring
spoon, scoop dough and roll into balls. Place
balls, 1 inch apart, on ungreased cookie sheets.
Flatten tops slightly.

4 Bake for 12 to 18 minutes or until deep golden
brown around edges. Cool on cookie sheet on
wire rack for 10 minutes. With spatula, transfer
cookies to racks to cool completely. Repeat with
remaining dough.

5 To assemble, brush flat sides of half of cooled
baked cookies with melted chocolate. Spread flat
sides of remaining cooled baked cookies with
marshmallow crème. Sprinkle with ⅛ teaspoon
salt. Sandwich cookies together. Refrigerate until
chocolate sets, about 2 hours.

EACH COOKIE: ABOUT 138 CALORIES, 2G PROTEIN,
15G CARBOHYDRATE, 8G TOTAL FAT (5G SATURATED),
0.5G FIBER, 26MG CHOLESTEROL, 99MG SODIUM.

Chocolate-Banana
WHOOPIE PIES

Bananas not only add great flavor to these fun treats,
they also make the chocolate cookies extra-moist.

ACTIVE TIME: 40 MINUTES   **TOTAL TIME:** 55 MINUTES PLUS COOLING   **MAKES:** ABOUT 20 COOKIES

2 cups all-purpose flour

2/3 cup unsweetened cocoa

1 teaspoon baking soda

¼ teaspoon salt

2 ripe bananas

⅓ cup sour cream

1 teaspoon vanilla extract

6 tablespoons butter or margarine, softened

1 cup sugar

1 large egg

1⅓ cups marshmallow crème

1 Preheat oven to 350°F. Line two large cookie sheets with parchment paper.

2 In medium bowl with wire whisk, combine flour, cocoa, baking soda, and salt. From bananas, mash enough for ½ cup; finely chop remaining and reserve. In another medium bowl, mix mashed banana, sour cream, and vanilla.

3 In large bowl with mixer on medium-high speed, beat butter and sugar until well combined. Beat in egg until well blended, occasionally scraping bowl with rubber spatula. Reduce speed to low. Alternately add flour mixture with sour cream mixture, beginning and ending with flour mixture; beat just until smooth, occasionally scraping bowl.

4 Drop 1 rounded measuring teaspoon batter onto prepared sheet. Repeat with remaining batter, spacing 2 inches apart. With wet fingertips, flatten tops of balls to form rounds.

5 Bake for 12 to 15 minutes or until centers spring back when lightly pressed, rotating cookie sheets between upper and lower racks halfway through baking. Cool completely on sheets on wire racks.

6 Turn half of cookies flat side up. Top each with 1 tablespoon marshmallow crème. Divide reserved chopped banana among centers of crème topping, then add remaining cookies sandwich-style.

EACH COOKIE: ABOUT 165 CALORIES, 2G PROTEIN, 29G CARBOHYDRATE, 5G TOTAL FAT (3G SATURATED), 2G FIBER, 20MG CHOLESTEROL, 105MG SODIUM.

Merry Meringues
(page 102)

6 Pressed, Piped, or Sliced

Here's your chance to grab a piping bag, cookie press, or knife, skip the fancy frosting, and create gorgeously shaped cookies full of holiday cheer. Choose a festive color and pipe our Merry Meringues into gorgeous swirls, press buttery dough into Cinnamon Stars topped with sparkling sugar crystals, or take your pick of slice-and-bake cookies studded with dried cranberries, apricots, or cherries.

Check the weather before baking delicate meringue cookies; if it's humid outside, they'll only collapse. If you plan to make meringues ahead, it's best they're kept at room temperature. Stash the cookies in metal tins (empty coffee cans work well) or self-sealing bags with the air pushed out, and they'll last for up to 2 weeks.

MERRY Meringues

A rainbow of colors makes these melt-in-your-mouth
cookies truly merry.

ACTIVE TIME: 20 MINUTES   TOTAL TIME: 1 HOUR 25 MINUTES PLUS COOLING   MAKES: 5 DOZEN COOKIES

3   large egg whites

Pinch salt

¼   teaspoon cream of tartar

½   cup granulated sugar

½   teaspoon vanilla extract

Assorted food coloring pastes

1   Arrange oven racks in top and bottom thirds
of oven. Preheat oven to 225°F. Line two large
cookie sheets with parchment paper.
2   In medium bowl with mixer on medium speed,
beat egg whites and salt until foamy. Add cream
of tartar; beat on medium-high until soft peaks
form when beaters are lifted. Sprinkle in sugar
1 tablespoon at a time, beating until sugar has
dissolved. Add vanilla and a flavor, if using

(see Your Color Code, below); continue beating
until egg whites stand in stiff, glossy peaks when
beaters are lifted.
3   For each color desired, using a small brush,
lightly paint 3 to 4 stripes of food coloring inside
large piping bag fitted with ½-inch plain tip.
Divide meringue among piping bags. Pipe meringue
into 1½-inch rounds onto prepared cookie sheets,
spacing 1 inch apart. Bake for 1 hour.
4   Turn oven off. Leave meringues in oven for
1 hour with oven door closed. Remove from oven;
cool completely.

EACH COOKIE: ABOUT 5 CALORIES, 0G PROTEIN,
2G CARBOHYDRATE, 0G TOTAL FAT, 0G FIBER,
0MG CHOLESTEROL, 10MG SODIUM.

Your Color Code

It's easy to add pizzazz to our Merry Meringues (above). Proceed with recipe as directed,
but in step 2, pick your food coloring paste and add a "matching" flavor from below:

- ½ teaspoon almond extract + green
- 2 teaspoons freshly grated lemon peel + yellow
- ½ teaspoon mint extract + red
- ¼ cup finely crushed freeze-dried blueberries + purple

Lemon Meringue DROPS

All the fabulous flavors of your favorite pie
have been miniaturized into melt-in-your-mouth morsels.

ACTIVE TIME: 20 MINUTES   **TOTAL TIME:** 1 HOUR 30 MINUTES PLUS COOLING
MAKES: ABOUT 5 DOZEN COOKIES

3 large egg whites

⅛ teaspoon salt

¼ teaspoon cream of tartar

½ cup granulated sugar

2 teaspoons freshly grated lemon peel

1 Arrange oven racks in top and bottom thirds of oven. Preheat oven to 200°F. Line two large cookie sheets with parchment paper.

2 In medium bowl with mixer on medium speed, beat egg whites and salt until foamy. Add cream of tartar; beat on medium-high speed until soft peaks form when beaters are lifted. Sprinkle in sugar 1 tablespoon at a time, beating until sugar has dissolved. Continue beating until egg whites stand in stiff, glossy peaks when beaters are lifted. Gently fold in lemon peel.

3 Spoon meringue into large piping bag fitted with ½-inch star tip. Pipe meringue into 1½-inch stars onto prepared cookie sheets, spacing 1 inch apart. Bake for 1½ hours or until meringues are crisp but not brown, rotating sheets between racks halfway through baking.

4 Turn oven off. Leave meringues in oven for 1 hour with oven door closed. Remove from oven; cool completely.

EACH COOKIE: ABOUT 5 CALORIES, 0G PROTEIN, 2G CARBOHYDRATE, 0G TOTAL FAT, 0G FIBER, 0MG CHOLESTEROL, 10MG SODIUM.

Tutti-Frutti Chewy
MERINGUES

These crisp meringue sandwiches, studded with dried pineapple, cranberries, and apricots, are filled with lemon curd.

ACTIVE TIME: 20 MINUTES   **TOTAL TIME:** 1 HOUR 25 MINUTES PLUS COOLING

MAKES: ABOUT 2½ DOZEN COOKIES

- ¾ cup dried pineapple, cut up
- ⅓ cup dried cranberries
- ⅓ cup dried apricots, sliced
- 2 teaspoons cornstarch
- 3 large egg whites
- Pinch salt
- ¼ teaspoon cream of tartar
- ½ cup granulated sugar
- ½ teaspoon vanilla extract
- ½ cup lemon curd
- 2 drops green food coloring

1 Arrange oven racks in top and bottom thirds of oven. Preheat oven to 225°F. Line two large cookie sheets with parchment paper.

2 In food processor with knife blade attached, pulse dried pineapple, dried cranberries, dried apricots, and cornstarch until finely chopped.

3 In medium bowl with mixer on medium speed, beat egg whites and salt until foamy. Add cream of tartar; beat on medium-high until soft peaks form when beaters are lifted. Sprinkle in sugar 1 tablespoon at a time, beating until sugar has dissolved. Add vanilla; continue beating until egg whites stand in stiff, glossy peaks when beaters are lifted.

4 With rubber spatula, gently fold dried fruit into meringue. Transfer meringue to large resealable plastic bag with corner snipped off. Pipe into 1-inch rounds onto prepared cookie sheets, spacing 1 inch apart. Bake for 1 hour; remove from oven. Cool completely on cookie sheets on wire racks.

5 To assemble, tint lemon curd with food coloring. Spread half of flat sides of cooled meringues with lemon curd mixture. Top with remaining cookies.

EACH COOKIE: ABOUT 90 CALORIES, 1G PROTEIN, 18G CARBOHYDRATE, 2G TOTAL FAT (1G SATURATED), 0G FIBER, 16MG CHOLESTEROL, 20MG SODIUM.

Chocolate-Almond
MERINGUES

Snow-white meringues get extra-fancy when dipped
in melted bittersweet chocolate and roasted salted almonds.

ACTIVE TIME: 40 MINUTES   **TOTAL TIME:** 2 HOURS 20 MINUTES PLUS COOLING AND STANDING
MAKES: 4½ DOZEN COOKIES

3   large egg whites

¼   teaspoon almond extract

⅛   teaspoon cream of tartar

Pinch salt

½   cup granulated sugar

¾   cup roasted salted almonds

5   ounces bittersweet chocolate, chopped

1   Preheat oven to 200°F. Line two large cookie sheets with parchment paper.

2   In medium bowl with mixer on high speed, beat egg whites, almond extract, cream of tartar, and salt until soft peaks form when beaters are lifted. Sprinkle in sugar 1 tablespoon at a time, beating until sugar has dissolved and egg whites stand in stiff, glossy peaks when beaters are lifted.

3   Spoon meringue into large resealable plastic bag with one corner cut to create small hole. Pipe meringue into 1-inch rounds, 1 inch apart, on prepared sheets.

4   Bake for 1 hour 30 minutes to 1 hour 40 minutes or until crisp but not brown, rotating cookie sheets halfway through baking. Cool completely on sheets on wire racks.

5   Meanwhile, in food processor with knife blade attached, pulse almonds until finely chopped; place on plate. Place chocolate in small microwave-safe bowl and microwave on medium (50% power) for 1 minute 30 seconds or until chocolate melts, stirring every 30 seconds.

6   Line large jelly-roll pan with waxed paper. Dip bottom third of each meringue into melted chocolate, then almonds, using fork if necessary to help hold meringue base when dipping. Place on prepared pan; let stand until chocolate sets.

EACH COOKIE: ABOUT 35 CALORIES, 1G PROTEIN, 4G CARBOHYDRATE, 2G TOTAL FAT (1G SATURATED), 0G FIBER, 0MG CHOLESTEROL, 10MG SODIUM.

Cranberry SHORTBREAD

These pretty slice-and-bake cookies are as tender and buttery as traditional shortbread. For photo, see page 11.

ACTIVE TIME: 35 MINUTES **TOTAL TIME:** 1 HOUR 25 MINUTES PLUS CHILLING AND COOLING
MAKES: ABOUT 5 DOZEN COOKIES

1   lemon

1   cup (2 sticks) butter, softened

1¼ cups confectioners' sugar

⅛   teaspoon salt

1   large egg

2¼ cups all-purpose flour

¾   cup dried cranberries

½   cup shelled pistachios, finely chopped (optional)

1 From lemon, grate 1 tablespoon peel and squeeze 1 tablespoon juice. In large bowl with mixer on medium speed, beat butter, sugar, and salt until smooth and creamy. Beat in egg, then lemon peel and juice, occasionally scraping bowl with rubber spatula. Reduce speed to low; beat in flour just until blended. Stir in cranberries until evenly distributed.

2 Divide dough among three sheets of waxed paper; roll each piece into 1-inch-diameter log. (If dough is sticky, refrigerate for 30 minutes before rolling.) Wrap logs in waxed paper and refrigerate for 45 minutes.

3 If using, divide pistachios among logs; press into dough to evenly coat. Wrap tightly in plastic wrap and refrigerate for at least 1 hour or until dough is firm enough to slice.

4 Arrange oven racks in top and bottom thirds of oven. Preheat oven to 300°F. Line two cookie sheets with parchment paper.

5 Working with 1 log at a time (keep remaining logs refrigerated), cut into ¼-inch-thick slices. Place slices, about 2 inches apart, on prepared cookie sheets. Bake for 25 to 30 minutes or until golden brown, rotating cookie sheets on racks halfway through baking. Slide parchment with cookies onto wire racks to cool completely. Repeat with slicing remaining logs and baking on cooled, newly lined cookie sheets.

EACH COOKIE: ABOUT 60 CALORIES, 1G PROTEIN, 7G CARBOHYDRATE, 3G TOTAL FAT (2G SATURATED), 0G FIBER, 11MG CHOLESTEROL, 35MG SODIUM.

Cinnamon STARS

These wonderful pressed cookies with warm spices
need only a sprinkling of colored sugar to add sparkle.

ACTIVE TIME: 25 MINUTES   **TOTAL TIME:** 1 HOUR PLUS COOLING   **MAKES:** ABOUT 10 DOZEN COOKIES

1   cup (2 sticks) butter, softened

1   package (8 ounces) full-fat cream cheese,
    softened

1   cup granulated sugar

1   teaspoon ground cinnamon

½   teaspoon ground ginger

½   teaspoon ground allspice

½   teaspoon salt

1   large egg yolk

1½ teaspoons vanilla extract

2½ cups all-purpose flour

¼   cup colored coarse sugar crystals

1 Preheat oven to 375°F.

2 In large bowl with mixer on medium-high
speed, beat butter, cream cheese, granulated
sugar, cinnamon, ginger, allspice, and salt until
light and fluffy. Beat in egg yolk and vanilla,
occasionally scraping bowl with rubber spatula.
Reduce speed to low; gradually beat in flour just
until blended, occasionally scraping bowl.

3 Spoon one-third of dough into cookie press.
Press cookies into star shapes onto large
ungreased cookie sheet, spacing about 2 inches
apart; lightly sprinkle with colored sugar.

4 Bake for 12 to 18 minutes or until deep golden
brown around edges. Cool cookies on cookie
sheet on wire rack for 10 minutes. With spatula,
transfer cookies to wire rack to cool completely.
Repeat with remaining dough and colored sugar.

EACH COOKIE: ABOUT 38 CALORIES, 0.5G PROTEIN,
4G CARBOHYDRATE, 2G TOTAL FAT (1G SATURATED),
0G FIBER, 8MG CHOLESTEROL, 27MG SODIUM.

Hot off the Press

To make our Cinnamon Stars (above) and Spritz Cookies (page 61), you'll need a cookie
press (or cookie gun). This handy tool includes a selection of decorative templates. Soft,
buttery dough is spooned into the press, then pushed through the template to form
a design. When filling the press, only spoon one-third of the dough at a time and be sure
to press the cookies onto a completely cooled cookie sheet.

Matcha SPRITZ

Matcha green tea powder is ground from the finest
Japanese tea leaves. It can be enjoyed as a beverage or as
a recipe ingredient, like in these buttery pressed cookies.

ACTIVE TIME: 15 MINUTES   **TOTAL TIME:** 40 MINUTES PLUS COOLING
MAKES: ABOUT 3 DOZEN COOKIES

½ cup (1 stick) butter, softened

½ cup granulated sugar

4 ounces full-fat cream cheese, softened

¼ teaspoon salt

2 ounces white chocolate, melted and cooled

1 large egg

1 teaspoon vanilla extract

1½ cups all-purpose flour

4 teaspoons matcha green tea powder

1 Preheat oven to 350°F. In large bowl with
mixer on medium speed, beat butter, sugar,
cream cheese, and salt until light and fluffy. Beat
in white chocolate, egg, and vanilla, occasionally
scraping bowl with rubber spatula. Reduce speed
to low; gradually beat in flour and tea just until
blended, occasionally scraping bowl.

2 Transfer dough to large piping bag fitted with
star tip. Pipe dough into 2½-inch-round wreaths
onto large ungreased cookie sheet, spacing
about 2 inches apart. Bake for 15 to 18 minutes
or until golden around edges. Cool cookies on
cookie sheet for 5 minutes. With spatula, transfer
cookies to wire rack to cool completely. Repeat
with remaining dough.

EACH COOKIE: ABOUT 75 CALORIES, 1G PROTEIN, 8G
CARBOHYDRATE, 4G TOTAL FAT (3G SATURATED), 0G
FIBER, 13MG CHOLESTEROL, 50MG SODIUM.

Chocolate-Almond
TEA COOKIES

These delicate finger cookies are dipped in bittersweet chocolate
and finely chopped almonds.

ACTIVE TIME: 25 MINUTES **TOTAL TIME:** 1 HOUR PLUS COOLING AND STANDING

MAKES: ABOUT 6 DOZEN COOKIES

1   cup (2 sticks) butter, softened

1   package (8 ounces) full-fat cream cheese, softened

1   cup granulated sugar

½   teaspoon salt

1   large egg yolk

1½ teaspoons vanilla extract

2½ cups all-purpose flour

5   ounces bittersweet chocolate, melted

½   cup slivered almonds, finely chopped

1 Preheat oven to 375°F.

2 In large bowl with mixer on medium-high speed, beat butter, cream cheese, sugar, and salt until light and fluffy. Beat in egg yolk and vanilla, occasionally scraping bowl with rubber spatula. Reduce speed to low; gradually beat in flour just until blended, occasionally scraping bowl.

3 Transfer dough to large piping bag fitted with large open star tip. Pipe dough into 2-inch logs onto large ungreased cookie sheet, spacing 2 inches apart.

4 Bake for 12 to 18 minutes or until deep golden brown around edges. Cool cookies on cookie sheet on wire rack for 10 minutes. With spatula, transfer cookies to wire racks to cool completely. Repeat with remaining dough.

5 Line large cookie sheets with waxed paper. Place almonds in small bowl. Brush ends of cooled baked cookies with melted chocolate. Dip chocolate ends into almonds. Transfer to prepared cookie sheets and let stand until chocolate sets, about 3 hours.

EACH COOKIE: ABOUT 75 CALORIES, 1G PROTEIN, 7G CARBOHYDRATE, 5G TOTAL FAT (3G SATURATED), 0.5G FIBER, 13MG CHOLESTEROL, 46MG SODIUM.

CRUNCHY
Candy Canes

Pretty enough to hang on the tree, these goodies
are as much fun to make as they are to eat.

ACTIVE TIME: 25 MINUTES   TOTAL TIME: 1 HOUR PLUS FREEZING AND COOLING

MAKES: ABOUT 3½ DOZEN COOKIES

1   cup (2 sticks) butter, softened

1   package (8 ounces) full-fat cream cheese,
    softened

1   cup granulated sugar

½   teaspoon salt

1   large egg yolk

1½ teaspoons vanilla extract

2½ cups all-purpose flour

Red or green food coloring

1   Preheat oven to 375°F.

2   In large bowl with mixer on medium-high
speed, beat butter, cream cheese, sugar, and salt
until light and fluffy. Beat in egg yolk and vanilla,
occasionally scraping bowl with rubber spatula.
Reduce speed to low; gradually beat in flour just
until blended, occasionally scraping bowl.

3   Tint half of dough with food coloring. Transfer
tinted dough to one side of large piping bag fitted
with small open star tip. Transfer remaining
plain dough to other side of piping bag. Pipe
dough into 2-inch-long candy canes on large
ungreased cookie sheet, spacing 1 inch apart.
Repeat as necessary. Freeze until firm, about 45
minutes.

4   Bake for 12 to 18 minutes or until deep golden
brown around edges. Cool cookies on cookie
sheet on wire rack for 10 minutes. With spatula,
transfer cookies to wire rack to cool completely.
Repeat piping, freezing, baking, and cooling with
remaining dough.

EACH COOKIE: ABOUT 105 CALORIES, 1G PROTEIN,
11G CARBOHYDRATE, 6G TOTAL FAT (4G SATURATED),
0G FIBER, 22MG CHOLESTEROL, 78MG SODIUM.

Cinnamon STICKS

These delicate cookies get their crunch from finely chopped pecans.

ACTIVE TIME: 40 MINUTES   **TOTAL TIME:** 1 HOUR 30 MINUTES PLUS CHILLING AND COOLING
MAKES: ABOUT 10 DOZEN COOKIES

3½ cups all-purpose flour

1   teaspoon baking soda

1   teaspoon ground cinnamon

1   cup (2 sticks) butter or margarine, softened

1   cup granulated sugar

1   cup packed brown sugar

2   large eggs

1   cup pecans, finely chopped

1   Line 9" by 5" metal loaf pan with plastic wrap, letting wrap extend on all sides. In medium bowl with wire whisk, combine flour, baking soda, and cinnamon.

2   In large bowl with mixer on medium speed, beat butter and sugars for 2 minutes or until light and fluffy, occasionally scraping bowl with rubber spatula. Add eggs, one at a time, and beat until blended. Reduce speed to low; gradually beat in flour mixture just until blended, occasionally scraping bowl. Stir in pecans.

3   Evenly pat dough into prepared pan. Cover and refrigerate for at least 4 hours or until dough is firm enough to slice.

4   Preheat oven to 325°F. Line large cookie sheet with parchment paper.

5   Invert dough onto cutting board; discard plastic wrap. Cut dough crosswise into ¼-inch-thick slices. Cut each slice lengthwise into ¼-inch sticks. Place sticks, 1 inch apart, on prepared cookie sheet. Bake for 12 to 13 minutes or until golden. Slide cookies, still on parchment, onto wire rack to cool completely. Repeat with remaining dough and cooled, newly lined cookie sheet.

EACH COOKIE: ABOUT 50 CALORIES, 1G PROTEIN, 6G CARBOHYDRATE, 2G TOTAL FAT (1G SATURATED), 0G FIBER, 8MG CHOLESTEROL, 30MG SODIUM.

TIP

Pulse the pecans in a food processor fitted with a knife blade until finely chopped.

Chocolate-Citrus
CRAN WHEELS

Chocolate and orange complement each other beautifully in these slice-and-bake cookies with dried cranberries.

ACTIVE TIME: 40 MINUTES **TOTAL TIME:** 1 HOUR 15 MINUTES PLUS CHILLING AND COOLING
MAKES: ABOUT 4 DOZEN COOKIES

2   cups all-purpose flour

¼   teaspoon baking soda

¼   teaspoon salt

¾   cup dried cranberries

½   cup confectioners' sugar

½   cup granulated sugar

¾   cup (1½ sticks) butter, softened

1   teaspoon freshly grated orange peel

1   teaspoon vanilla extract

¼   teaspoon ground cinnamon

12 ounces white or dark chocolate, melted

Dried orange slices, optional

1 In medium bowl with wire whisk, combine flour, baking soda, and salt. In food processor with knife blade attached, pulse cranberries, confectioners' sugar, and granulated sugar until cranberries are very finely chopped; transfer to large mixing bowl.

2 In large bowl with mixer on medium-high speed, beat cranberry mixture and butter until combined. Beat in orange peel, vanilla, and cinnamon. Reduce speed to low; gradually beat in flour mixture just until blended, occasionally scraping bowl with rubber spatula. Divide dough in half. Roll each half into a 2-inch-diameter log; wrap tightly with plastic wrap. Refrigerate overnight or until dough is firm enough to slice.

3 Preheat oven to 350°F. Line large cookie sheet with parchment paper.

4 Working with 1 log at a time, cut into ¼-inch-thick slices. Place slices, about 1 inch apart, on prepared cookie sheet. Bake for 15 to 17 minutes or until golden brown around edges. Let cool on cookie sheet for 5 minutes. Slide parchment with cookies onto wire rack to cool completely. Repeat with slicing remaining log and baking on cooled, newly lined cookie sheets.

5 Dip cooled cookies halfway into melted chocolate, if desired, and place on waxed paper-lined cookie sheet. Decorate with orange slices, if desired. Refrigerate until chocolate sets.

EACH COOKIE: ABOUT 100 CALORIES, 1G PROTEIN, 14G CARBOHYDRATE, 5G TOTAL FAT (4G SATURATED), 1G FIBER, 8MG CHOLESTEROL, 50MG SODIUM.

PB & J PINWHEELS

Pinwheel cookies are a holiday favorite. Our delicious version
is a combo of peanut butter dough and raspberry dough.

ACTIVE TIME: 30 MINUTES   **TOTAL TIME:** 1 HOUR PLUS CHILLING AND COOLING
MAKES: ABOUT 5 DOZEN COOKIES

2¾ cups all-purpose flour

½ teaspoon baking soda

¼ teaspoon salt

1   cup (2 sticks) butter or margarine, softened

1   cup granulated sugar

1   large egg

1   teaspoon vanilla extract

⅔ cup creamy peanut butter (sweetened, no-stir variety)

½ teaspoon raspberry extract

1   bottle (0.25 ounces) red food coloring

1 In medium bowl with wire whisk, combine flour, baking soda, and salt.

2 In large bowl with mixer on medium speed, beat butter and sugar until light and fluffy. Add egg, vanilla, and ⅓ cup peanut butter; beat until well mixed. Reduce speed to medium-low; gradually beat in flour mixture just until blended, occasionally scraping bowl with rubber spatula. Transfer half of dough to large bowl. To one bowl of dough, add raspberry extract and red food coloring, beating until well incorporated. Into other bowl of dough, with rubber spatula, stir in remaining ⅓ cup peanut butter.

3 Between two 20" by 15" sheets of parchment paper, roll peanut butter dough into 15" by 12" rectangle. Repeat with raspberry dough. Refrigerate both rectangles until chilled but still pliable, about 10 minutes.

4 Remove top sheets of parchment from both rectangles. Invert one rectangle onto other so edges line up evenly, trimming if necessary. Remove top sheet of parchment. Starting from long side, tightly roll rectangles together, peeling back bottom sheet of parchment while rolling. Cut log in half. Wrap each half in plastic wrap. Refrigerate for at least 1 hour or up to 3 days, until dough is firm enough to slice.

5 Arrange oven racks in top and bottom thirds of oven. Preheat oven to 350°F.

6 With knife, cut logs crosswise into ¼-inch-thick slices. Place slices, 1 inch apart, on two large ungreased cookie sheets. Bake for 10 to 12 minutes or until golden brown, rotating cookie sheets between upper and lower racks halfway through baking. With spatula, transfer cookies to wire racks to cool completely. Repeat with remaining dough and cooled, newly lined cookie sheets.

EACH COOKIE: ABOUT 80 CALORIES, 1G PROTEIN, 8G CARBOHYDRATE, 5G TOTAL FAT (2G SATURATED), 0G FIBER, 11MG CHOLESTEROL, 62MG SODIUM.

TIP

Tightly wrap the logs of dough and freeze for up to 2 weeks. To bake, transfer the logs to the refrigerator for 30 minutes or until soft enough to slice.

Gingerbread WANDS

Our thoroughly modern take on gingerbread cookies
has all the wonderful taste you expect, thanks to pumpkin pie spice.
(Psst! We also add a hefty pinch of black pepper.)

ACTIVE TIME: 30 MINUTES **TOTAL TIME:** 45 MINUTES PLUS COOLING **MAKES:** ABOUT 7 DOZEN COOKIES

½ cup granulated sugar

½ cup light molasses

1 tablespoon pumpkin pie spice

¼ teaspoon ground black pepper

2 teaspoons baking soda

½ cup (1 stick) butter, melted

1 large egg

3½ cups all-purpose flour

1 large egg white, beaten

Colored sugar crystals, edible glitter, and sprinkles (all available at wilton.com), optional

1 Preheat oven to 325°F. Line large cookie sheet with parchment paper.

2 In 4-quart saucepan, combine granulated sugar, molasses, pumpkin pie spice, and black pepper; heat to boiling over medium heat, stirring occasionally. Remove from heat; stir in baking soda, then melted butter. With fork, stir in egg, then flour until combined.

3 On floured surface, knead dough until smooth; divide in half. Wrap 1 piece dough in plastic wrap and set aside. With lightly floured rolling pin, roll remaining half of dough into 12" by 8" rectangle (should be about scant ¼-inch thick). With pizza cutter, cut dough into ¼-inch-wide, 8-inch-long strips. Transfer to prepared cookie sheet, spacing about 1 inch apart.

4 Lightly brush strips with egg white. Sprinkle with colored sugar, glitter, and sprinkles, if desired. Bake for 12 to 15 minutes or until set. Slide parchment with cookies onto wire rack to cool completely. Meanwhile, repeat rolling, cutting, and decorating with remaining dough on cooled, newly lined cookie sheets.

EACH COOKIE: ABOUT 45 CALORIES, 1G PROTEIN, 8G CARBOHYDRATE, 1G TOTAL FAT (1G SATURATED), 0G FIBER, 5MG CHOLESTEROL, 40MG SODIUM.

PRESSED, PIPED, OR SLICED

Almond Macaroon
FINGERS

Almond paste is what keeps these treats extra moist and chewy.

ACTIVE TIME: 30 MINUTES   TOTAL TIME: 50 MINUTES PLUS COOLING AND STANDING
MAKES: ABOUT 3½ DOZEN COOKIES

1   tube or can (7 to 8 ounces) almond paste

½   cup confectioners' sugar

2   large egg whites

½   teaspoon vanilla extract

2   ounces bittersweet or semisweet chocolate, melted

1 Arrange oven racks in top and bottom thirds of oven. Preheat oven to 300°F. Line two large cookie sheets with parchment paper.

2 In food processor with knife blade attached, process almond paste and sugar until combined (a few small lumps will remain). Add whites and vanilla; pulse until well combined.

3 Spoon batter into piping bag fitted with ½-inch star tip. Pipe batter into 3-inch-long fingers onto prepared cookie sheets, spacing 1 inch apart.

4 Bake for 17 to 19 minutes or until cookies start to turn golden brown on edges, rotating cookie sheets between upper and lower racks halfway through baking. Cool cookies completely on cookie sheets on wire racks. Repeat with remaining dough and cooled, newly lined cookie sheets.

5 With pastry brush, brush chocolate on half of each macaroon. Place on waxed paper. Let stand until chocolate sets.

EACH COOKIE: ABOUT 35 CALORIES, 1G PROTEIN, 5G CARBOHYDRATE, 2G TOTAL FAT (0G SATURATED), 0G FIBER, 0MG CHOLESTEROL, 3MG SODIUM.

TIP

If necessary, place cookies the in refrigerator for 5 minutes to set the chocolate.

CHRISTMAS Jewels

Candied pineapple and red and green cherries give these buttery cookies their gem-like appearance. The logs of dough can be refrigerated for up to 1 week before slicing.

ACTIVE TIME: 40 MINUTES **TOTAL TIME:** 1 HOUR 30 MINUTES PLUS CHILLING AND COOLING
MAKES: ABOUT 10 DOZEN COOKIES

1 cup (2 sticks) butter, softened

1 cup confectioners' sugar

1 large egg

2¼ cups all-purpose flour

½ teaspoon salt

⅓ cup red candied cherries

⅓ cup green candied cherries

⅓ cup diced candied pineapple

1½ cups pecans

1 In large bowl with mixer on medium speed, beat butter and sugar for 2 minutes or until light and fluffy, occasionally scraping bowl with rubber spatula. Reduce speed to low; beat in egg until blended. Gradually beat in flour and salt just until blended, occasionally scraping bowl. With spoon, stir in candied fruits and ½ cup pecans.

2 Cover bowl with plastic wrap and refrigerate dough for at least 2 hours or until firm enough to shape. Meanwhile, finely chop remaining 1 cup pecans.

3 Divide dough in half; shape each half into 9" by 2" inch log. Spread half of chopped pecans on 13-inch-long sheet of waxed paper. Roll 1 log in pecans, gently pressing to coat. Wrap log tightly in waxed paper. Repeat with remaining pecans and dough on second sheet of waxed paper. Refrigerate logs for at least 3 hours or until dough is firm enough to slice.

4 Preheat oven to 350°F. Line large cookie sheet with parchment paper. Remove 1 log from refrigerator; cut crosswise into ¼-inch-thick slices. Place slices, 1 inch apart, on prepared cookie sheet. Bake for 12 to 13 minutes or until golden around edges. With spatula, transfer cookies to wire racks to cool completely. Repeat with remaining dough and cooled, newly lined cookie sheets.

EACH COOKIE: ABOUT 70 CALORIES, 1G PROTEIN, 7G CARBOHYDRATE, 4G TOTAL FAT (2G SATURATED), 0G FIBER, 10MG CHOLESTEROL, 45MG SODIUM.

PRESSED, PIPED, OR SLICED

Index

Photography Credits

COVER (front and back):
Mike Garten

© Monica Buck: 42, 46

Deposit Photos: © Artstudio Pro 21; © Elenathewise 37

Getty Images: © Aleaimage 115; © Meike Bergmann 67; © DNY59, 32;
© Douglas Johns 10; © Ian O'Leary 41; © Smneedham 34

iStockphoto: © Agorohov 72 (left); © Ajafoto 126 (left); © Kaan Ates 45;
© Basilios1 126 (right); © Dionisvero 72 (right); © Eivaisla 61; © G215 111;
© Richard Griffin 81; © InaTs 31; © Juanmonino 62; © Mattjeacock 51;
© MizC 76; © Tatyana Nikitina 103

© Yunhee Kim: 28, 52, 65, 60, 80, 90, 107

© Kate Mathis: 11, 17, 24, 38, 49, 83, 89, 105, 119, 120

Kate Mathis: 6, 74, 92

© ANDREW MCCAUL: 15, 18

© Marcus Nilsson: 44, 68, 113

© Con Poulos: 99

Shutterstock: © Scott Bolster 19

Stockfood: © PhotoCuisine /Jean-Claude Amiel 59; © Paul Poplis 21

Studio D: Chris Eckert 7; Mike Garten 2, 12, 54, 84, 94, 100, 110, 116

Metric Conversion Charts

The recipes that appear in this cookbook use the standard United States method for measuring liquid and dry or solid ingredients (teaspoons, tablespoons, and cups). The information on this chart is provided to help cooks outside the U.S. successfully use these recipes. All equivalents are approximate.

METRIC EQUIVALENTS FOR DIFFERENT TYPES OF INGREDIENTS

STANDARD CUP	FINE POWDER (e.g. flour)	GRAIN (e.g. rice)	GRANULAR (e.g. sugar)	LIQUID SOLIDS (e.g. butter)	LIQUID (e.g. milk)
¾	105 g	113 g	143 g	150 g	180 ml
⅔	93 g	100 g	125 g	133 g	160 ml
½	70 g	75 g	95 g	100 g	120 ml
⅓	47 g	50 g	63 g	67 g	80 ml
¼	35 g	38 g	48 g	50 g	60 ml
⅛	18 g	19 g	24 g	25 g	30 ml

USEFUL EQUIVALENTS FOR LIQUID INGREDIENTS BY VOLUME

¼ tsp	=							1 ml
½ tsp	=							2 ml
1 tsp	=							5 ml
3 tsp	=	1 tbls	=			½ fl oz	=	15 ml
		2 tbls	=	⅛ cup	=	1 fl oz	=	30 ml
		4 tbls	=	¼ cup	=	2 fl oz	=	60 ml
		5⅓ tbls	=	⅓ cup	=	3 fl oz	=	80 ml
		8 tbls	=	½ cup	=	4 fl oz	=	120 ml
		10⅔ tbls	=	⅔ cup	=	5 fl oz	=	160 ml
		12 tbls	=	¾ cup	=	6 fl oz	=	180 ml
		16 tbls	=	1 cup	=	8 fl oz	=	240 ml
		1 pt	=	2 cups	=	16 fl oz	=	480 ml
		1 qt	=	4 cups	=	32 fl oz	=	960 ml
						33 fl oz	=	1000 ml = 1 L

USEFUL EQUIVALENTS FOR DRY INGREDIENTS BY WEIGHT

(To convert ounces to grams, multiply the number of ounces by 30.)

1 oz	=	1⁄16 lb	=	30 g
4 oz	=	¼ lb	=	120 g
8 oz	=	½ lb	=	240 g
12 oz	=	¾ lb	=	360 g
16 oz	=	1 lb	=	480 g

USEFUL EQUIVALENTS FOR COOKING/OVEN TEMPERATURES

	Fahrenheit	*Celsius*	*Gas Mark*
Freeze Water	32° F	0° C	
Room Temperature	68° F	20° C	
Boil Water	212° F	100° C	
Bake	325° F	160° C	3
	350° F	180° C	4
	375° F	190° C	5
	400° F	200° C	6
	425° F	220° C	7
	450° F	230° C	8
Broil			Grill

USEFUL EQUIVALENTS LENGTH

(To convert inches to centimeters, multiply the number of inches by 2.5.)

1 in	=					2.5 cm		
6 in	=	½ ft	=			15 cm		
12 in	=	1 ft	=			30 cm		
36 in	=	3 ft	=	1 yd	=	90 cm		
40 in	=					100 cm	=	1 m

THE GOOD HOUSEKEEPING
TRIPLE-TEST PROMISE

At *Good Housekeeping*, we want to make sure that every recipe we print works in any oven, with any brand of ingredient, no matter what. That's why, in our test kitchens at the **Good Housekeeping Research Institute**, we go all out: We test each recipe at least three times—and, often, several more times after that.

When a recipe is first developed, one member of our team prepares the dish, and we judge it on these criteria: It must be **delicious**, **family-friendly**, **healthy**, and **easy to make**.

1   The recipe is then tested several more times to fine-tune the flavor and ease of preparation, always by the same team member, using the same equipment.

2   Next, another team member follows the recipe as written, **varying the brands of ingredients** and **kinds of equipment**. Even the types of stoves we use are changed.

3   A third team member repeats the whole process **using yet another set of equipment** and **alternative ingredients**. By the time the recipes appear on these pages, they are guaranteed to work in any kitchen, including yours. **We promise**.